Charles John Vaughan

My son, give me thine heart

Sermons preached before the Universities of Oxford and Cambridge, 1876-1878

Charles John Vaughan
My son, give me thine heart
Sermons preached before the Universities of Oxford and Cambridge, 1876-1878

ISBN/EAN: 9783744735896

Printed in Europe, USA, Canada, Australia, Japan

Cover: Foto ©Lupo / pixelio.de

More available books at **www.hansebooks.com**

SERMONS

PREACHED

BEFORE THE UNIVERSITIES OF OXFORD
AND CAMBRIDGE.

MY SON, GIVE ME THINE HEART:

SERMONS

PREACHED

BEFORE THE UNIVERSITIES OF
OXFORD AND CAMBRIDGE,
1876—1878.

BY

C. J. VAUGHAN, D.D.

MASTER OF THE TEMPLE,
AND CHAPLAIN IN ORDINARY TO THE QUEEN.

London:
MACMILLAN AND CO.
1878

[*The Right of Translation is reserved.*]

CONTENTS.

SERMON I.

SCORN A BREACH OF THE SIXTH COMMANDMENT.

PAGE

MATTHEW v. 22. Whosoever shall say, Thou fool, shall be in danger of hell fire 1

SERMON II.

THE SYMPATHY OF GOD A NECESSITY OF MAN.

MARK iv. 38. Master, carest Thou not that we perish? 33

SERMON III.

A NARROW PLACE—AND NO TURNING.

NUMBERS xxii. 26. A narrow place, where was no way to turn either to the right hand or to the left . 61

SERMON IV.

INDIVIDUAL INDEPENDENCE A COROLLARY OF REDEMPTION.

PAGE

1 CORINTHIANS VII. 23. Ye are bought with a price: be not ye the servants of men 93

SERMON V.

ONE THING THOU LACKEST.

MARK x. 21. Then Jesus beholding him loved him, and said unto him, One thing thou lackest . 129

SERMON VI.

AN HUNDREDFOLD NOW IN THIS TIME.

MARK x. 29, 30. There is no man that hath left house, or brethren, or sisters, or father, or mother, or wife, or children, or lands, for my sake, and the Gospel's,

But he shall receive an hundredfold now in this time, houses, and brethren, and sisters, and mothers, and children, and lands, with persecutions; and in the world to come eternal life 161

SERMON VII.

THREE TYPES OF CHARACTER—ENTHUSIASM, RELUCTANCE, COMPROMISE.

                                                   PAGE

LUKE IX. 62. No man, having put his hand to the plough, and looking back, is fit for the kingdom of God 197

SERMON VIII.

THE PROPER ATTITUDE FOR RELIGIOUS ENQUIRY.

PSALM CXXXI. 2, 3. I do not exercise myself in great matters, which are too high for me.
    But I refrain my soul, and keep it low . . 231

I.

SCORN A BREACH OF THE SIXTH COMMANDMENT.

SCORN A BREACH OF THE SIXTH COMMANDMENT.

MATTHEW v. 22.

Whosoever shall say, Thou fool, shall be in danger of hell fire.

WE have here an example of the legislation of Jesus Christ. His kingdom must have its laws. This necessity is not superseded either by the freeness of the grace which saves, or by the freedom of the life into which it gives entrance. The Christian man has no thought of meriting either the favour of God now or the acceptance of God hereafter. But the very fact that he is saved by grace implies that he is to walk in newness of life; and for instruction in the meaning of that word *newness* he must look to the Lord of the *life*—to Him who has said, in reference not only to the mysteries of the future but to the duties of the present, *Behold, I make all things new.*

The forgiven man needs instruction. For want of it, though it lies there in the Gospel—for want of it, though to prayer and meditation it would unfold itself in minute direction—for want of it, though the Saviour lives to minister the Spirit, and casts out none who come to Him—he lives immeasurably below the standard of the great confession, stumbles day by day along a path which might bask in light, and pays the penalty in a thousand regrets and remorses which make a perpetual demand upon the treasury of the inexhaustible grace.

Now the legislation of Jesus Christ might have taken an altogether new departure. It might have begun with new terms and new definitions: it might have discarded existing rules, and struck out a path for itself, in which the words "grace" and "spirit" and "love" might have taken the place of all mention of particular sins and particular duties. Such a course might have been more evidently original: it might have brought to an earlier or more direct issue the conflict between Law and Gospel: it might have been more satisfactory, at first sight, to persons whose bitter experience recorded the weakness of nature and of the Fall in the face of commands and prohibitions addressed to an erect posture and a free will.

But no reader of the Gospels, no student of the Sermon on the Mount, can say that our Lord passed the sponge over existing systems, and avowed His intention to subvert either natural or revealed religion as He found it ready to the hand of a Teacher come from

God. In His first and most systematic discourse upon Divine and relative duties, He takes the Decalogue as His subject; selects some of its separate commandments for comment and illustration; and shows the operation upon it of a higher law of life, in which the letter is subordinated to the spirit, but which makes no pretence of replacing the actual and the practical by anything that is unreal, visionary, or transcendental.

The Decalogue was the transcript of natural duty; expressing, in strong bold outline, what man owes as a creature to his God, and as a fellow-creature to his fellows. This law can never be superseded: but it may be illuminated, it may be transfigured, it may be breathed upon and breathed into and re-inspired by its Author.

Not to destroy, but to fulfil, was the office of Christ towards the law and the prophets. Not to demolish, but to fill—not to take down the fabric of the old, but to bring into it the presence which shall occupy each chamber with a life at once Divine and most human—this is the legislation of Jesus Christ, and the text is one of its most beautiful and characteristic examples. He comes to rescue this commandment, the sixth of the Decalogue, from the literalism of the Scribe, from the fantasticality of the Pharisee, and to lift it into the spirituality—the thoroughness, that is, and the practicalness—of the new, the Gospel life.

He begins by bringing together (as in some following instances) the commandment and the gloss. The strong sturdy prohibition, *Thou shalt not kill*—one of the ten thunders of Sinai, so stern and tremendous that *they who heard entreated that no word might be added*—had fallen into the manipulating hands of a later Rabbinism, and received the feeble appendage of a literalizing enactment, *And whosoever shall kill shall be liable to the judgment.* Thus translation might hesitate, not without apology, between the "to" and the "by" in this Greek dative. *It was said* to *them of old time* is true of *Thou shalt not kill. It was said* by *them of old time* might suit better the clause about liability to the judgment. We have, indeed, if we examine it, not one, nor two, but three speakers, in the sentences here before us. There is the Divine word—there is the human gloss—there is the God-Man interpreting the one and removing the other. God spake, man added to it, *but I say unto you.*

We pause for a moment upon the majesty of the claim here advanced. It is the assertion of a right to supersede all human authorities: it is the assertion of a right to stand side by side in authority with the Divine Legislator Himself. The Divinity of Jesus Christ waits not, as some would persuade you, for later developements; waits not even for the fourth Gospel and for the Evangelist St John. It breathes in each page of the first Gospel; in the Sermon on the Mount, with its *I say unto you;* in the Parable of the Tares, *The Son of Man shall send forth His Angels...The field, His field, is the world;* in the revelations of the last day, *The Son of Man shall sit on the throne of His glory...and before Him shall be gathered all nations.*

Whosoever shall kill shall be in danger of the judgment. The nearest court of resident Levites shall sit in judgment on him, and shall condemn. This was all that the Scribe had to say upon this sixth statute of the Decalogue. All was dull bare prose: there was the crime, and there was the punishment—the act done and that which came of it. Who troubled himself to go deeper? Who busied himself about the sin, when he had dealt with the crime? Who cared to dive into the depths of the heart, who cared to penetrate into the recesses of the life, and interest himself about the poor disconsolate creature of God that had sinned and must die? Still more, who cared to draw out of his sad record something that should be of use to fellow-men, to keep them off the shipwreck-rocks which had been death and hell to men of one blood and of one nature with themselves?

Not the Scribe nor the Pharisee. Their little office was magnified when they had settled who should sit upon this case, and where. But Jesus Christ—*the Man of sorrows, acquainted with grief*—could He stop there? Did He not care who sinned, or who died for it, provided the court were correct, the process exact, the punishment certain? Therein lies the difference between Him and them. *I judge no man. I came to save the world.* And to save is to forewarn. Beware then of this or that within thee which will drive thee upon this quicksand.

I say unto thee, interpreting the sixth commandment of the Decalogue, *Whosoever is angry with his brother*—yes, *his brother,* if he is a man—he has committed murder. Anger is murder. Cautious scribes have interpolated here the reservation, *without a cause*[1]; just as other scribes have inserted *easily* before *provoked* in the Divine pæan of Charity[2]. They recalled, perhaps, the saying, *Be ye angry and sin not;* and thought that moral indignation ought to be expressly exempted from the condemnation of anger. But moral indignation needs no such saving clause. Moral indignation never shed blood; or, if it did, it was not murder. No, the anger of which Christ speaks under the head of killing, is, of course, sinful anger. Let the local court, let the seven Levites, or the three and twenty Levites, deal with that.

But the peculiarity, the originality, of our

---

[1] The εἰκῇ of the received text is at least *doubtful.*
[2] See 1 Cor. xiii. 5, οὐ παροξύνεται.

Lord's statute of murder, lies *here;* not in the mention of anger, but in the *Raca* and the *Moré* which follow it.

Anger is *of course* unchristian. The lowest court can judge of that. There is no need to carry its questions to the capital. The justice-room of the nearest borough can deal with them. Not because they are trivial, but because they are obvious. Who does not see that selfish, violent, ungoverned anger is a breach of the sixth commandment when Christ's light is let in upon it? Let us go on—let us go deeper. Let us go to the *Raca*, and the *Moré*.

The word *Raca* has had several interpretations. It may mean—it probably does mean—"empty" or "silly." Some have found for it a more precise application. They have given it the sense of one who errs in doctrine, and have found encouragement for this suggestion in the reference of the case to the council or Sanhedrin. Some have gone on to take *Fool* in its occasional derived sense of *Atheist*. *The fool hath said in his heart, There is no God*. And thus we should have that climax of insult of which we hear too much in these days; and the man who calls his brother *Raca* will call him *Heretic*, and the man who calls his brother *Fool* will call him *Atheist*, and we shall have a graduated scale of affront and calumny, by no means indeed imaginary or unreal, but introducing perhaps one of those too exact, too antithetical parallels, which forget the dignity of the Divine Speaker in the smartness and sharpness of a human repartee.

We may not be able accurately to distinguish, by shade of colour, the *Raca* from the *Moré*. Enough that they are distinguished in the word of truth before us. Lighter, less harsh, less contemptuous, evidently, the one is than the other. We can all feel a difference—there is one—between calling a man Simpleton and calling a man Fool. We can imagine our Lord saying, Whosoever shall say *Simpleton* shall (in Gospel antitype) go before the Sanhedrin: it is an offence against love, an offence therefore against the God of love—it shall not go unpunished. Whosoever shall say *Fool* shall go straight (in Gospel antitype) to the Gehenna, the valley of Hinnom, in which idolatrous Israelites once sacrificed to Moloch, and which a royal Iconoclast defiled afterwards with burnt bones of men.

Never let us strain Holy Scripture, the words of Jesus Christ, into a rigid compliance with rules of artificial rhetoric. Let us acquiesce in a climax less than perfect in an antithesis less than startling. There is a wisdom above man's wisdom even in the *foolishness*—an Apostle has gone before us—*the foolishness of God*, as well as a strength above man's strength in His weakness.

This we can see—and it is enough—that between the first example and the second of the motives of murder we have passed from one region, from one climate, into another. And if between the second example and the third it is not so; if the *Raca* and the *Moré* are separated rather by degree than by kind; if a gulf is fixed between the one and the two, and but a hair's breadth be discernible between these two; yet is our moral clear, and our guidance certain: we have passed from the motive of anger into the motive of contempt, and the two contempts are at least distinguishable, while the fact that *Scorn can kill* is brought out with terrible emphasis in the combination of the two.

To make Scorn worse than Anger in the region of malevolent passion—at all events, to hunt the malevolent passion from the covert of wrath into the cavern of contempt—is at once an instructive lesson, and a striking feature of the Gospel. It was said to the ancients, as they quaked before the mountain of the terrific Presence, *Thou shalt not kill.*

But I *say unto* you, the Church bought with my blood, *Whosoever shall say to his brother, Raca, shall be liable to the council; and whosoever shall say, Fool, shall be in danger of hell fire.*

We are not to suppose that it is the *word* "fool" which is the thing really prohibited. Such an interpretation would be an example of that Pharisaism against which the text itself is directed. Christ Himself used the word. *Ye fools and blind* was one of His own appellations of the Rabbis of that day. This indeed would not of itself sanction our use of it. He who knew what was in man had a right to all words—and to this amongst them. There is here before us an instance of the power of the Bible—of our own English Bible— upon the language and upon the conscience of the people. The word of this text is under a ban. Men who do not think much of Jesus Christ, men whose conscience is not sensitive to right and wrong, pay an unconscious homage to the prohibition of one particular term of contumely; would shrink from using, would not be suffered to use in decorous society, one to another, the arrogant, the insolent, the exasperating word *Fool.* But it is of the thought rather than the word that our Lord speaks. Whosoever shall *think* of his brother *Thou fool* shall be a transgressor, shall be a murderer, in the eye of God.

There is no scorn in the Gospel. It might be said indeed, Is there then unreality? is there complaisance? is there flattery? is there a double tongue and a false pretending? How, without this, can I help thinking *Thou fool* of half the men and the women who meet me in society?

We are not to call folly wisdom, any more than we are to put darkness for light, or sweet for bitter. It is implied everywhere in the Bible that there is a diagnosis of folly possible;

that we are not intended to be credulous, to be promiscuous, to be either blind or false, in our observation of character or in our intercourse with mankind. There is a truthfulness of seeing and estimating, there is an instinct, and a duty also, of self-preservation, which presupposes a sort of judgment upon characters, and without which it would be idle to have it written in Scripture—it is one text amongst many to a like purpose—*He that walketh with wise men shall be wise, but the companion of fools shall be destroyed.*

But who does not feel that this is a different thing altogether from scorn?

Scorn is, first, arrogance, and then cruelty.

It is the second of these which gives it its place here, as a breach, in spirit, of *Thou shalt not kill.*

But even this rises out of the other. Cruelty itself is first pride. What enables thee to injure thy brother? What makes it possible, makes it endurable, to thee, to make that other life wretched, or to stamp it out? What but that thou art greater and nobler, more valuable and more necessary, than that other? Who stops to ask himself, What have I that I did not receive? who made me thus, and another thus? Scorn forecloses such questionings: the *thou fool* in the heart makes the life selfish and the dealing disdainful.

Yes, there is a deeper thing than anger even in the slaying. The wrath would not rise, for some wrong done to the self-love, for some standing in the way of my interest, or of my honour, or of my love, for some supposed slight put upon me, or affront offered, or rivalry threatened, if there were not first in me that idea of importance, that notion of superiority, that conceit of self, of which the natural vocative for the other being is, *Thou fool.* Then the self-thwarted becomes the self-avenger, and the little insignificant unimportant life must go down before the one which is so large and so essential.

Thus it is that the prohibition before us ranges itself under the statute of murder. Scorn is murder. Witness the examples of which India under English rule is fertile. The ruling race, in its heart, says *Fool* to the native. The arrogant thought cherished becomes insolence, becomes violence, becomes homicide, under provocation, and marvels if it must be tried for it. But why cross the seas for our examples? Where is not the contemptuous thought ready to be oppression, ready to be murder, if it had scope? That superfluous, that trivial, that inferior life, what matters it? let me insult it, let me trample upon it, let me put it out, if it is very much, or very obstinately, in my way.

We have sought to bring into view the first meaning of the precept—its connexion with the sixth commandment—its investigation of the motives of murder. But we feel, as we speak, that there is a deeper truth and a yet more instructive lesson behind.

Anger and contempt point towards murder, while we think only of the body. But is not He who thus traces murder to its source enlarging also its definition? It might seem to require some ingenuity to connect the red hand of the murderer with the inward thought of the heart, *Thou fool*. But not so when we think what it is, in Christ's sight, to kill. Not when we remember His own saying, *Fear not them which kill the body*. There is something else which can be killed. There is the life's life of the man. There is the bright vigorous intellect, ever bracing itself for new marches and new conquests, and needing for their achievement an atmosphere in which it can breathe, and a sky under which it can enjoy. There is the warm loving heart, eager for affection, quick to offer, quicker to respond;

the heart of which sympathy is the life and coldness the destruction. There is the informing, animating, quickening soul; the thing in each one of us which struggles upward, makes for the light, wills the good, feels the force of right, accuses itself for its failures, rises or would rise from its falls, feels that it has a purpose in being, would not perish without having done its work, would not be extinguished till it has both shone and kindled, would not depart hence till it knows the *whither* and the *to whom*. Surely when our Lord Jesus Christ made the *Raca* and *Moré* murderers, He was teaching a new lesson as to the real and the unreal killing. He was elevating our idea of life and death, quite as much as He was showing how contempt, no less than anger, may prompt to homicide.

In this point of view, how instructive becomes the prohibition of so much as the thought,

Thou fool. What is it which depresses and beats down the intellect, when it would march and learn and know? Who are the unsuccessful teachers, the inefficient lecturers, in our Schools and Universities? Are they not the conceited self-satisfied men, who cannot put themselves even in imagination on the level of the learner, who make him feel himself accosted as a fool, and by being so accosted made so? Who are they to whom we owe the earliest and (after all) the most substantial acquirements, the very tools and implements of all subsequent progress, of all later attainment? Who but the loving sister or mother who fostered the nascent intellect by an encouragement which put growth into it?

And what is it which stunts and dwarfs and deforms the yet higher life in all of us, the life of feeling and the life of love? What is it which has sometimes turned the generous warm-hearted boy into a fastidious, discontented, loveless misanthrope? What but the contempt with which his earliest tenderness was treated by the being upon whom it was lavished not wisely but too well?

But what is it which kills the soul—longing to live the life which hath immortality, longing to receive, longing to communicate, blessing? Is it not this—the calm quiet *Thou fool* which just looks at us the evil eye; which silently, civilly, courteously implies the ridiculousness of our even attempting, even wishing, to be either this or that to any one living thing that moves or creeps or crawls upon this earth? Or, if we look within, and think not of the desire to benefit, but of the soul's hunger and thirst after righteousness; is it not, here again, scorn—scorn not spoken but given to be understood—which quenches, inside us, the smoking flax of grace, the spirit for brave resolve, the trust in One not against but for us? Who is it that helps me to be better? Is it not the man who believes in me—or, if this cannot quite be, the man who expects, the man who hopes, for me? Yes, the man who knows or makes room for my poverty, my ignorance, my fault, my sin, yet, because He also knows of a love stronger than hate, and a strength prevalent in weakness, feels, and lets me feel, that there is an omnipotence in the self-despair?

We see then, by the opposite, that the man who thinks scorn of me is maleficent towards me if not malevolent; that he who so much as thinks at me *Thou fool* may be the murderer in me of that which is my life.

The Scripture precept makes no exception when it says, *Honour all men.* It counsels not unreality, complaisance, or flattery. It says not, There is in all men something to admire, something to compliment, something of which to say, *It is good, it is beautiful, let it alone.* But it says this, There is no living thing—made to live, kept in life, by the Self-existent and the All-wise—to which any other living thing shall be justified, shall be even true, in saying *Contemptible* or in saying *Fool*. In each living man there is something to honour, were it but the fact that he hath his life from God. In each there is something to respect, could we but find it; something to hope for, could we but discern it; something to work from, could we but get at it. Were it but the misfortune of home or education, of circumstance or companionship, of temperament or temper, of defective powers or mind deformed, surely the more privileged, the more advantaged, ought rather to honour than to contemn. This it is which makes ministry possible; yea, the ministry of the dying bed, or the ministry of the condemned cell. The image of God, discoloured, defaced, sin-stained, sin-corroded, is there still, beneath all; beneath the wickedness, the cunning, the falsehood and filthiness, of a whole life of sinning: and it is the secret, it is the power also, of the God-taught, instead of scorning, instead of saying to this lost brother, *Thou fool*, to find out that image, and to make it find out itself.

Suffer, brethren, the word of exhortation. Wherever there is power, wherever there is advantage, there is the capacity at least, and the temptation, of scorning. Our Lord addressed Himself to no imaginary, no improbable, audience, when He bade His disciples to beware, as they loved Him, of the rising thought of scorn. We have called it the temptation of power; yet with equal truth it might be called the very touchstone and criterion of weakness. The young schoolboy can despise his fellow for having a less fleet foot or a less cunning hand than his own; can even make a mock at the halting gait of the cripple, or the faltering speech of the paralytic. He lives to learn the unkindness, the ungenerousness, the unmanliness, of such contempts: the growth of real strength corrects instead of fostering the self-conceit of inexperience. It ought to be thus in all things. It ought to be thus with all contempts: they ought to be outgrown with the growth of the man; they will be so with the growth of the real man— the man of mind and heart, of soul and spirit. But this growth is often capricious, often intermittent; and infantine, babyish judgments survive into full stature and even into hoar hairs.

There is a scorning which parades itself in smart writing, and which recommends a tone of contempt as an accomplishment of the intellectual. There is an affectation of sneer and sarcasm, but too easily caught, and but too attractive to the young. There is a quick eye for the ludicrous, and a ready tongue for satire, and a lively imagination to extend the bounds of the ridiculous till the landmark is removed altogether between profane and sacred, which are irresistibly alluring to some natures, infinitely more sparkling and more impressive than the speech of simple truth and the judgment of honest charity.

Even they who rise above these coarser influences of the scorner have a danger of their own in that very superiority. How severe oftentimes is the verdict of a moral young man upon a weaker or less disciplined comrade. How little mercy does he show to the promise which comes to nothing, to the effort which failed to succeed, to the faint hand which (in Scripture phrase) *smote thrice and stayed*. How readily does he pronounce upon the hopelessness, the good-for-nothingness, of a character which yet has to live out its days, and has to go afterwards to the judgment. Let him lay to heart the warning of Jesus Christ, that he who says to his brother, *Raca* or *Fool*, may even be that brother's slayer. These are just the severities which make hell enlarge herself. Let the brother of firmer mould and more established virtue be the helper and not the sentencer of the lagging dallying companion. The day may come, even to him, when he shall find his own utmost strength *like the tow when it toucheth the fire* in the face of some yet invisible influence which shall try his very life of what sort it is.

But not virtue alone, religion also, has its scorning. We can understand, we can respect, if we cannot sympathize with, every honest conviction of doctrine or ritual: we cannot respect the arrogance which makes another an offender for a word, catches at the mispronunciation of some Shibboleth of Protestantism, or looks down upon a hair's breadth departure from the tradition of a (so called, but often self-styled) Catholicism. It is the *Raca* and the *Moré*, in these matters, which

THE SIXTH COMMANDMENT. 31

bewray them: right or wrong in themselves, they are wrong certainly in the positiveness and in the disdain.

Whosoever shall say, Thou fool, shall be in danger of hell fire.

O, if the Eternal Son, O, if the Holy Spirit of God, had said to fallen man, lying in his vice and lying in his ruin, *Thou fool*, where had been hope, where had been redemption? Jesus Christ saw in him the Father's handywork, knew that the Creator could re-create, and came forth from Him to do it. The Holy Ghost saw the ruined being lifted and re-created, yet needing the perpetual presence, the unwearied indwelling; and though the thing to be indwelt was hospital and prison and mad-house in one, He hesitated not to give up the two millenniums or the six millenniums of a Divine Heaven, that He might wrestle with the obdurate, and, one by one, bring again the lost.

And the Father—the Holy and Almighty yet most merciful Father—He was in the One, He was in the Other; He gave, He sent; He sympathizes, and He will save; and thus the precept, *Thou shalt not kill*, becomes the fact, *This my son was dead and is alive*—Angels in heaven are enabled to sing a new song over sinners repenting, and one man after another falls on the long sleep, saying, *I know whom I have believed: I shall be satisfied, when I awake, with Thy likeness.*

Divine scorn is a contradiction in terms: let us make it to be so with the human.

II.

THE SYMPATHY OF GOD A NECESSITY OF MAN.

II.

THE SYMPATHY OF GOD A NECESSITY OF MAN.

Mark iv. 38.

Master, carest Thou not that we perish?

In a dangerous storm on the capricious inland sea of Gennesaret, a little boat, occupied by thirteen persons, is crossing from the Western to the Eastern shore. The waves are beating into the ship, so that it is now full of water: and One, evidently the Leader of the little company, is in the hinder part of the vessel, not helping, not cheering, not sympathizing with the rest; no—asleep. It is He who suggested the crossing; He, who, when the evening of a long toilsome day was come, had said, *Let us pass over unto the other side.* In some sense, then, He was to blame for the peril. Why had He not foreseen the winds and the waves, and postponed the voyage at least till the morning? They had trusted Him—not wisely but too well: and now, instead of feeling for them in their distress, He lies there taking His rest; lies there asleep. The sting of the danger is in that sleep. If He were awake, and alive to their trouble, they could have borne it. They were always ready to follow Him; sometimes they thought they could die with Him. But that He should be indifferent to their alarm, that He should be able to sleep through it, this was unkind, this was unlike Him. Half in astonishment, half in reproach, they at last awaken Him with the question, *Master, carest Thou not that we perish?*

Miracle and parable are but differences of name in many places of the Gospels, and it is so here. That crossing, that storm, that sleep, that awakening, all were typical: real as facts, significant as emblems. They have all been acted again and again in human lives, in spiritual histories. Redemption itself is just that—a world's misery, a world's sense of neglect, a Divine sleep, a Divine awakening: *the times of that ignorance God winked at*, at last He interposed for deliverance, rebuked the wind and the sea, and would have all men everywhere to be saved.

Master, carest Thou not that we perish? is one of those graphic and pathetic touches which we owe to this second Gospel. The other Evangelists are contented to say, *Master, Master, we perish;* or, *Lord, save us; we perish.* St Mark, preserving (it may be) a reminiscence of St Peter, who was himself present on the occasion, gives that which we seem to recognize at once as the exact expression; represents, at all events, the precise point of the feeling, in this *Carest Thou not?* is it nothing to Thee whether we live or die? hast Thou no thought for us who have left all for Thee?

There can be no doubt that, even amongst human beings, it is an immense aggravation of any calamity to feel that it is not cared for. To suffer unregarded, neglected, unloved, with cold careless eyes looking on, or closed in idle sleep which one touch of sympathy would have prevented, is a thing differing in kind as well as degree from any suffering which has love or even pity as its companion.

The expostulation of Gethsemane, *Couldest not thou watch with me one hour?* was the utterance (in part at least) of a human distress. Made in all things like unto His brethren, the Man of sorrows was expressing in that pathetic interrogation the very thought breathed once, with apparent but only apparent reason, to Him, *Carest Thou not that we perish?* Even He, proving in all things His Deity by His

Humanity, was human also in this, that He accepted, that He even yearned for sympathy, and could say, in the agony of the sin-bearing, to one from whom He might have looked for compassion, Carest thou not for this *horror of great darkness,* for this fear of death which is fallen upon me?

All have known at some time the double sadness of a bereavement which, for any reason or for none, has lacked sympathy. Sometimes there has been a character veiled from all but its very nearest and dearest. Surrounding friends, even friends near as a brother, have not been admitted to the privacy, or have not been congenial to the disposition, of the person whose departure has created, just for one heart, a perpetual desolation. And how has it jarred upon that one heart to hear the vague condolences, to receive the inadequate, the half unreal, lamentations, of those who compassionate indeed, but cannot sympathize with the individuality of the orphanage or the widowhood which must go with the one mourner to the grave!

Thus is it in all experiences: we see it even in the vilest. The hisses and execrations, even the curses not loud but deep, of a condemning mob, have had power to add bitterness to the last horrors of a public execution. For these have been the infallible evidences that no man compassionates; that over those fathomless, those gloomy waters, there plies no vessel of commiseration. These have brought home to the dying criminal the awful conviction—more awful than any death—that no man cares that he perishes.

On the other hand, there is no fear and no anguish and no form of death which may not be soothed and mitigated by the presence of a generous, heart-deep, selfless sympathy. It is no stretch of imagination to hope, that some softening influence may have communicated itself to the hearts of those shipwrecked mariners of yesterday, in the sight of pier and beach swarming with agonized beholders, powerless indeed to help, but strong to feel, and assuring them by look and sign that there were those who cared if they perished. And it is no imagination at all, but the simple record of certainty, that those brave miners of a Welsh valley, whose very names are become within these last weeks household words for England, found hunger itself assuaged by the first sound of hands and voices busy for their deliverance; found in the being cared for, long days ere that caring could ensure the rescue, a relief from the chief horror, of desertion and desolation, such as bore up through nine days of suspense the sinking spirits, and would have made death itself less than intolerable, just by reason of the same peculiarity of human nature, to which indifference is the sting of suffering, and sympathy the very life of life.

It is this known instinct of nature which

makes the last offices of nurse and physician, of pastor and friend, so powerfully ministerial to the bed of inevitable, inexorable death. It is this which has added the last touch of misery to deaths died in abandonment or exile, where there has been none to catch the last sigh, to breathe the name of home, or to point the eye and the heart upward to that opening heaven where the Son of Man standeth at the right hand of God.

But in the instance before us there was a more than human sympathy missed and craved for. And thus it carries our thoughts into a region above that of earthly brotherhood, and suggests some reflections, not unsuitable (I trust) to the occasion, upon the complaints and expostulations of humanity itself in the ear of *a God that hideth Himself* and a Saviour seeming to slumber.

It cannot be denied that there are many facts and many experiences in the life of this world, which irresistibly suggest the question whether God can be waking, or, if wakeful, caring. To try to enumerate such phenomena is as needless as it would be painful. We cannot but read this sleep of Jesus Christ, in the boat tossed by the waves, with His disciples standing by, wondering and half murmuring, as intended to represent the world-wide agelong mystery to which we are pointing.

It does seem wonderful, not only or chiefly that there should be pain, disease, and death, in the earth—earth being what it is in the matter of sin: for we cannot but feel that it would be more wonderful still, a real offence to faith, a real stumbling-block to virtue, if a sinful were not also a suffering creation: but how, in the confession of the Book of God itself, all the foundations of the earth are thrown out of course by the existence of sin upon it, and by the perversenesses, mismanagements, and self-contradictions, which are the growth and fruit of that primary fact of evil. *Carest Thou not*, we are tempted to say to the Divine Ruler Himself, that, whether it be by a moral murder or by a moral suicide, we Thy creatures are perishing?

And even if this mystery of the existence of evil were explained or palliated, it would still be wonderful how evil should be allowed to spread and diffuse itself, where there was either no freedom of choice on the part of its victim, or even a will to resist if the strength were but present. We see the ancestry of evil, tainting to remote generations an offspring which had nothing left for its inheritance but the memory of crime and sorrow. We see a leprosy of shame and vice corroding the very walls of houses, in which nevertheless women and children must drag out their miserable being, though to do so is to be involved in consequences of which they are not originators but victims. Nay, we see, here and there, efforts made, difficulties encountered, battles waged, in the vain endeavour of some helplessly entangled life to rid itself of those fetters of evil which it had no share in riveting. How can all this be—we vex ourselves with the question—if indeed there is a God at once of holiness, love, and power, superintending, ruling or even overruling, a world which He caused to be and which He keeps in being? *Carest Thou not*, we find ourselves asking, as we suffer or as we look on, *Carest Thou not that we perish?* Is it possible that neither the violence, nor the malignity, nor the blasphemy, of wicked men should evoke the interference, were it but for the protection of the innocent, of a God living and waking, a God on the side of right, and a God resistless in power?

These questions are as old as the Fall, and we have learned in some measure the lesson of patience concerning them. But when the experience comes into a man's own life, he finds himself still asking, *Carest Thou not that I perish?* Painful it might still be to suffer—pain and suffering are but names for each other—painful it must be to live uneasy days, in body or spirit, through poverty and its circumstances, through disease and loneliness, through fears and fightings on spiritual subjects, through cavils of doubters, and taunts of scoffers, and all the thousand tortures of a busy and inventive infidelity: painful this must be, whatever its shape and form: yet even this is not the worst thing. If I could see in all this a kindly purpose, an end and an aim, like that spoken of by the Patriarch, *When He hath tried me, I shall come forth as gold,* I could bear anything. I can understand that I want a sharp discipline, of scourge and cross, to cure me of my levity and my vanity. I can understand that I want earth's lamps darkening, one by one, to make the light of heaven precious or even real to me. The dreadful, the intolerable thing is, to be left alone in this process; to be allowed to fancy myself the sport of chance, the plaything of destiny; to see no hand guiding and no finger pointing anywhither, and therefore to be constantly driven, by stress of searching winds and lashing waves, to look towards the unseen Presence, and say, *Carest Thou not that I perish?*

We might go still further, and say that the sympathy of God is more vital to us even than His Omnipotence. The disciples *accepted* the perishing—in other words, the non-intervention of Christ to save: what they could not accept was His not caring. In its influence upon the heart, to care is more than to save. Love is more than power, even in the Divine. We must not make light of any one of the attributes: it is the combination of *all* the attributes which indeed forms our very conception of God. To suppose God all else, and yet limited in point of power, cannot seriously be allowed without robbing ourselves of His Deity. But it is permissible to go all lengths in pressing one by one upon our hearts all His perfections. And to-day we have before us His sympathy. We are dwelling upon the thought how essential it is that He should care for us; how absolutely nothing can make up to us for the absence of that care. Far better would it be for us, as spiritual and immortal beings, to imagine that there might be some opposing and thwarting impediment in the way of the present exercise of God's attribute of Omnipotence, than that there should be any defect or any coldness in His love. If we could believe that the true explanation of the present confusion was this, that the power of evil, though doomed, is not yet actually subdued and subjugated to the might of God; that there is a real warfare going on, such as the Apocalypse paints to us, between two empires of light and darkness—that, so far from being asleep or being indifferent, God is conducting a campaign, as for defeat or victory, against the united rebel forces of dragon, beast, and false prophet; and that, though the final issue is certain, the last field is not yet fought, nor captivity yet led captive—this would go far to reconcile us to the conditions and the experiences of the present; for it would at least secure to us His lively wakeful sympathy with every soul's struggle and every life's agony of our own: it would explain to us, as far more than a parable, that revelation of joy in heaven over each sinner that repenteth, of ministering spirits sent forth thence to watch over the heirs of salvation: it would lay to rest, thoroughly and for ever, that bitterest and cruellest of all suspicions, *Master, carest Thou not that we perish?*

And when a man has made up his mind, at all costs, to believe in the Divine care for him—and when we say, "at all costs," we mean at the cost of supposing some temporary limit to the present exercise of the Divine power itself—he will find, as he casts himself, day by day, upon that love and that compassion, that, for him at all events, however it may be for the universe, the power is already sufficient too. He may still be unable to add one jot or one tittle to the old arguments about the existence of evil; he may count it more reverent, as well as more true, to say, *Such knowledge is too wonderful for me, I cannot attain to it;* but he will find that the difficulty is no longer, for him personally, a moral difficulty; he will find that prayer does bring him the needed comfort and the needed help—as his day, so his strength is—beginning with the axiom, *Thou, God, carest*, he passes on into the experimental conviction, *There is none like unto Thee, O Lord: there is not one that can do as Thou doest.*

This is the present privilege of all who, for good or ill, cast in their lot decisively with Jesus Christ. Though for these, as for others, the theory of life is still dark and baffling, the practice is like the light shining more and more till the perfect shall come. On the hypothesis (as men speak) of the Gospel, the reading of the great riddle is but a question of time. For each particular life committed to it the mystery is unveiled already. *Yet a little while, and He that cometh shall come*, makes patience, patience and hope, patience, hope, and courage, these three, the sum and substance, the sufficient stay also, of the life that is. For others it is not so. On the life that has undertaken itself, its own charge, its own guidance, its own solution, the shadow lies heavily, and must lie, and the sun goes down in gloom. Whatever may be the eventual consolation of the race, that life has placed itself outside it. It has no evidences to add to the stock of hope, it has no encouragements to carry to the account of patience. To it the one only enquiry must be that of the text. As it marks the deepening anxieties of men and nations—as it hears of tottering faiths and despairing deathbeds—as it watches for the morning that comes not, and elaborates constitutions, Divine and human, which refuse to march, it can but look upward into the inscrutable impersonal heaven, and ask, Thou, if there be One in hearing—if all be not vague chance, shifting change, or inflexible law—if there be any One above, intelligent however silent, *carest Thou not that we perish?*

The question might have been asked with some force of reason—may be propounded still for such as believe not—were it not for that Divine intervention of which we have but just passed from the annual commemoration. The very reckoning of our years, little as we may notice it, reproves and forbids the expostulation of the *not caring*. It may be possible to exaggerate—certainly to misrepresent—the effects, as already realized on earth, of the Incarnation of our Lord Jesus Christ: it is impossible to overstate the argument of the sympathy and of the love. We may marvel at the slow march of the Gospel towards the conquest of nations, at the backward steps, here and there, of its beneficent influences, at the re-gathering of clouds of sin and misery once dispelled, at the imperfect success, everywhere, of that message of peace and holiness which ought by this time to have spread a new life over the face of the whole earth. We may feel—and we ought to feel—the responsibility of this failure as lying individually upon all who profess, but do not live, the Gospel. We may go so far as to say that mankind is still perishing, though the light of day has searched out the chambers of imagery, and made it no longer excusable to sit or to walk in darkness. Like the disciples on the sea of Galilee, we may feel ourselves in jeopardy, the Gospel having failed to work in us its saving work, and rather revealing than dispersing the gloom of sin and death.

One thing we cannot say—that our Master cares not. If He had not cared to save, would He have left the glories of Heaven to be born of a woman, to be made one of us, to share our weaknesses, temptations, and sorrows, to be despised and rejected by His own, to stoop at last to death, even the death of the Cross? Certainly He cares if we perish. Say, if you must say it, with the scoffer, that He attempted the impossible, that He miscalculated the comparative forces of antagonist good and evil, that He failed in His great adventure, that He lived and died in vain. Say, if you must say it, with the scoffer, that He was conscious of failure, that He felt Himself defeated, that He died broken-hearted. At least you cannot accuse Him of not caring. He took it upon Him to deliver man, He came upon earth, He endured the contradiction of sinners, He submitted to the last agonies, that He might help, that He might redeem, that He might regenerate, those who cared not for one another, those who cared not for themselves.

And though we can, if we will, perish in spite of Him—though a salvation by force is no salvation, and a soul that will slay itself can, and a fallen nature can always remain so, or sink lower and lower by successive acts of willing till it reaches that awful, that mysterious ruin to which Holy Scripture gives the name of *the second death*—this need not be. The salvation of Jesus Christ is a sufficient salvation—*to the uttermost* is its watchword—not by force, nor in spite of us, but with the consent of a will made willing, He can justify and sanctify, He can strengthen, and bless, and save.

If ever He should seem to sleep through our sorrows, or to be indifferent to our prayers, this is but to try our faith, to sober our lightness, to quicken our earnestness: soon will He arise and rebuke the wind and the sea: at last, for one and for another, He maketh the storm a calm, so that the waves thereof are still.

Carest Thou not? has a voice for the disciple as well as for the Lord. It reproves the lazy loitering, the purposeless sauntering, the silly dreaming, in which so many of us pilgrims and voyagers pass this responsible, this anxious lifetime. Not to care that we perish is suicide—not to care that our brother perishes is murder. Christ cared, God cared, that we might care: and yet, as I look within, as I look around me, I find almost nothing that expresses, almost nothing that is consistent with, this anxiety. I see lives given to this one thing, the making themselves easy and soft and luxurious. I see minds relaxing themselves by every sentimental, sensational, sensual study. I see souls, not so much bravely encountering questions of doubting, on purpose that they may know and on purpose that they may judge, but rather indolently suspending everything, as though doubt were wisdom—as though it were an evidence of power to be fertile in cavilling, cruel in unsettling. O if we would be thoughtful! O if we would be considerate! O if we would work! O if we would care!

"Give me one serious man" was the French statesman's challenge. "Give me one," we will echo it, "who cares if he himself—cares if his brother—perishes."

Standing this day on the margin of an undiscovered future; hearing Jesus Christ say to us this morning, *Let us cross to the other side;* knowing, yet not knowing, what that *other side* means—a condition, at all events, of mind and heart, different from, yet made by, the present—let us gather all our energies for the mystic, the allegorical crossing. Let us resolve, like the disciples before us, two things —that we will obey the summons as His, and that we will take Him with us. This if we do, we need fear no evil; no, not if the weeks of this Term should contain in them the transition from health to sickness, from life to death.

No stranger can visit unmoved those solemn memorials, of marble slab or painted window, which keep fresh in your Cathedral Church the loved names of young men called suddenly, by accident or fever, from amidst the energetic movements of Academical life into the stern realities of an everlasting hereafter. They live still—there, and here: there, we trust, resting, serving, knowing, learning, worshipping, aspiring; here, in salutary admonition for those that come after, bidding them to be ready always, remembering their Creator in the days of their youth.

This may be, for any one of us, *the other shore* to which Christ to-day is calling us: it may be so, even if no one thinks it.

But at all events change will be busy in this Congregation, even within the short space of one Term. O how many may have passed, by a few short steps, from faith to scepticism, from prayer to silence, from comparative innocence to a guilty conscience! Who can pretend to be confident, who can dare to be light-hearted, as he launches forth to-day for a shore veiled in mist, over a sea big with storm?

Let us all thank God that there is One who cares if we perish. Let us pray Him so to keep us in every going out and coming in— so to watch over us in the hours of toil, of converse, of resting—so to order all things for us, study, thought, influence, companionship—that we may never perish, but continually grow in grace and in the knowledge of Himself our Lord and our God.

III.

*A NARROW PLACE—AND
NO TURNING.*

III.

A NARROW PLACE—AND NO TURNING.

NUMBERS xxii. 26.

A narrow place, where was no way to turn either to the right hand or to the left.

THE goal is in view. Balaam is approaching the city of Balak. The waste road begins to be bordered by vineyards, and the vineyards are exchanged for the narrowing lanes and alleys of the suburbs. All is well. The first scruples of conscience, the preliminary objections of religion, the troublesome warnings of the night vision, have been successfully surmounted; and now the famous diviner, with his convoy of princes, sees before him, in near prospect, the rewards, in wealth and honour, of his exciting enterprise. Nothing can now hinder, nothing can long postpone, the royal favour, the national gratitude, for which he has suffered something and risked his all. There is a flutter of elation, an intoxication of delight, proper—peculiar, I had almost said—to that victory of the worse self over the better. The struggle is over, the die is cast, the offended conscience hides its wrath in its tent, the after-taste of bitterness, the hell of remorse, bides its time and follows after. We are in the pleasant pause between the lusting and the sinning, not in the painful pause between the sinning and the suffering.

It was thus, we imagine, with Balaam, as he rode forward that day with God's license (as he read it) to *go with the men.* We shall not enter to-day—for our purpose is different—into the character of this strange being—this wonderful compound and mixture of a man—or into the ethics of God's dealing with him. Writers and preachers have dwelt in all times upon the history of Balaam, as it stands forth on the sacred page in its mingled mystery of scruple and daring, of a heart-purpose of sinning and a conscientious reluctance to sin without permission. We see in Balaam the type of all who (in the phrase of a later Scripture) first set up their idol and then come to the prophet; who first put a stumbling-block before them and then enquire of God how not to stumble. Such a man gets his answer, short and sharp, from the oracle of those *first thoughts*, which in matters of duty are commonly far more trustworthy than the second. *Thou shalt not go with the men. Thou shalt not curse the people, for they are blessed.* He gives up the journey. But there is a restless querulous longing, which, though it has given up the journey, has not given up the lusting nor the murmuring. New messengers, *more, and more honourable*—new solicitations, stronger and more imperious—are allowed to re-open the question; and then conscience, which has spoken once plainly, shall speak the second time in riddle and almost by contraries. *If the men come, rise up and go with them.* Whose was the fault if that second answer was penal? Who was it who treated God as though He were such an one as himself, and thought to win by importunity a license which had been refused to simple enquiry?

Brethren, this third Sunday after Easter brings before us, in the new order of Lessons, the marvellous episode of Balak and Balaam; a mere enigma, as to its spiritual import, in many congregations—but in this congregation vocal, eloquent, monitory, alike to the elder and to the younger. I take one single point in the narrative, and it cannot be expressed more forcibly than in the words read as the text.

Three several times the Angel has stood in the way; impressing the awe of his apparition upon lower natures, upon irrational creatures, only not upon its human scope and object. What a parable of the insensibility of sin—how it renders a man blind to sights, and deaf to sounds, which are visible and audible to any one and anything that is innocent! *The dumb ass* pays the homage of fear to its Maker. Only the prophet—only *the man whose eyes are open, who hears God's words and sees the vision of the Almighty*—he alone is deaf and blind. Why? Because the spell of a sin is upon him. Is it not written, *According to Thy fear, so is Thy wrath?* The thing done, the thing meditated, may have displeased the Lord: the anger may be astir, the wrath may be powerful: to use the prophetic imagery, the deep may utter his voice, the right-aiming thunderbolts may be abroad, the sun and the moon may stand still in their habitation: yet the sinner can sin with a light heart through all, because he who fears not God regards not God's anger. The brute beast saw where the seer saw not. Instinct ranks below reason: yet instinct uncorrupted is above reason corrupted, even in its perspicacity, even in its intuition. If reason will debase herself—will use (she need not) her prerogative and privilege of sinning—then the steed and the rider change places instantly in intelligence, and the morbid subtlety of the rational sinks, even in range of vision, below the unsophisticated simplicity of the animal. The dumb ass sees what Balaam sees not.

But the patience of the Divine Antagonist is not yet exhausted. Once, twice, and thrice, He goes forth to withstand. Now the adversary *goes further, and stands* at last *in a narrow place, where there is no way to turn either to the right hand or to the left.* This will be a decisive battle. No longer able to *turn aside into the field,* or to *thrust herself unto the wall,* the ass now *falls under Balaam*—and yet he sees nothing. The eye so cunning in its foreview of destiny, so keen to descry the coming fortunes of Edom and Amalek, is dim and blind to the personal vision, to the Champion whose controversy is with *him.* Not till *the Lord opens the eyes of Balaam* can he discern the Angel in the way, and the drawn sword in his hand.

Yet why that drawn sword? Do you suppose that God fears the malediction of that soothsayer upon the chosen people? Could any words from that sin-clouded soul do injury, against the will of God, to the march of that cause which had in it, however veiled and shrouded, the world's welfare and the salvation of mankind? Surely we read here the will of God that not one sinner should perish; His merciful pleading with a man bent on his own ruin; His special intercession with a man of great gifts, that he turn them not into woes and into curses; but also His gracious dealing with men of all sorts and of all times, through the countless instrumentalities of Providence and of the Holy Ghost.

A narrow place, where was no way to turn either to the right hand or to the left. That is my parable.

It will scarcely be denied that there is in all of us a sensitive shrinking from what may be described as the coming to close quarters with God Himself.

It is so, first and above all, in the *soul*. A twilight life satisfies us. That middle thing, between night and day, is the utmost of our faith and of our hope. We have settled nothing. Nothing is beyond the reach of doubt. I cannot go forth with this weapon or with that, for I have not proved it. Suspense is my best. I have not given up Christ. I have not decided against the Atonement, or the Resurrection, or the Judgment. I have not made up my mind that there is no Holy Spirit, or no Christ, or no God. O no! Sometimes I am half persuaded that there is: then I doubt again. Meanwhile nothing passes, or can pass, within me, between my soul and its God, on the basis of revelations which to me are peradventures. My spiritual life is of necessity a blank. My worship, in secret or in the congregation, is a mere concession and compromise. I am terrified lest enquiry should land me in infidelity, and therefore I pacify myself, I lead a quiet life, by the help of a few forms. I keep infidel books shut; I expel Atheistical doubts as intruders; I speak slightingly or condemningly of unorthodox writers, lest I should be shaken, or distressed, or suspected, and in the hope that a respectable Christianity may last my time.

Who shall tell in how many cases the attraction of multiplied Sermons and Services, in how many cases the attraction of charitable employments and religious Societies, in how many cases the attraction of controversial reading and semi-secular preaching, lies just here; namely, in the shelter thus afforded to a condition of real distance and aloofness from God Himself? That disease to which nothing can effectually minister but a resolution of the man's own will to break through at all costs every dividing barrier, and to deal with God as a real Person whom to know is eternal life, is soothed and palliated, to a heart ill at ease, and a conscience not yet laid on sleep, by a multiplication of observances which are a tribute (at least) to religion, and of activities bearing the likeness (at least) of the Christian. Still the direct dealing tarries: *the narrow place* of the personal encounter is not yet reached.

These are *soul's* avoidances of the Divine contact. Others are of the *life*.

Many are they whose one struggle it is to

elude decision. While they can *turn aside*, into field or vineyard, from the obstructing Angel in the highway, it is well with them. They would settle no matter. That which presents itself in the light of duty paralyzes them. To do, or to leave undone, because it is right, and for no other reason, principal or subordinate, whatsoever, is an offence to them. It is inconvenient, it is discourteous, it is uncivil, for anything to address them in that tone. Many questions of duty, these say—as the former said, all questions of faith—are not to be faced, they are to be encompassed. *Edom said, Thou shalt not go through—wherefore Israel went round.* They will not encounter the question, whether this which they do is right, lest they should be constrained to forego it. All the world does it: it would be eccentric, it would be arrogant, to be singular: take it for granted. This is the history of all dishonesties in trade, and of all laxities in Professions. It is not only in the region of belief, it is quite as much in the province of action, that we dwell amidst a multitude of open questions. We do every day a number of things, about the wisdom or unwisdom, about the right and the wrong of which we are in suspense. We let them pass for the present: some day we will settle them. The whole detail of our lighter and less serious employments, the whole sphere of relaxation, of society, of expenditure of time on amusements and of money on self-indulgences, is this uncertain, conjectural, haphazard world for thousands. Meanwhile we follow the multitude—to do good, or to do evil.

These postponements of determination involve consequences. They lead to a desultory, vacillating, shambling life, if not to the one thing worse. A thoughtful man feels that even mistakes, even errors of judgment, are less serious than that sort of life which is the accident of an accident. Without affecting a judicial solemnity on every small particular of doing or not doing, he makes up his mind upon a few principles, says nothing about it, but keeps them till he finds better. The opposite character disparages rules, has no wish to be consistent in trifles, would rather live from hand to mouth in things insignificant, and sometimes wins applause or conciliates liking by the loose easy way in which he deals with the little moralities which are so influential in their bearing upon the general colour of the life.

Nor is it only in small things that this indecision reveals itself. Human life is full of it in reference to the gravest realities of sin and duty. Men who are both orthodox in opinion and unimpeachable in dealing may yet exemplify this very duplicity in that secret existence which lies altogether (we are fond of saying) between a man and his Maker. It is the very definition of bosom sins. They are sins kept back from God as much as from man. They are often, indeed, prayed against—even as Balaam could not let his avarice be unmentioned between him and God—but their peculiarity is, that somehow we always get leave for them. Either they are so trivial, or so natural, or so powerful, or so very very pleasant, that they must have indulgence. We could not go on with religion at all, if it was sternly severe with them. We like Christianity itself—it is a fearful thing to utter—because, read as we read it, it seems to hold out a hope of countless forgivenesses: at last, at worst, of a deathbed repentance.

Now God is the Adversary of all these subterfuges. He must be so. It is half the work of the Bible so to present Him. His attribute of Truth makes Him so. His attribute of Holiness makes Him so. His attribute, above all, of Love makes Him so. When we start on our journey, having persuaded ourselves that we have His license for sinning, He must—or He would not be God—*go forth to withstand.* The drawn sword is very terrible, but it is more than armistice or olive-branch if we will have it so. God wills not the death of the sinner, and therefore He must meet him while it is day.

It is as though He sought us first of all in places where we might evade Him. That face-to-face inevitable encounter is so terrible that He would spare us if we will let Him. Many a *smiting of the steed,* and many a *crushing of the foot,* is witness to these minor, these avoidable meetings. Yes, we are angry with friend and menial, we show discontent in our countenance, and visit it upon our companions, when we have a suspicion that God is out in our way, and that He is against us. The gentlest admonition, the tenderest hint of warning, suffices to rattle up the sleeping lions of pride and wrath against the innocent one beside us, who meant nothing but love.

And yet the longsuffering of God is not ended. He would have won us or He would have enticed us back—but we would not. Now He must *go further*.

I cannot express, as I would, the lifelikeness of the story. Not all the profane jests which have been lavished on it have made it less solemn to me or less sacred. This *narrow place*, what is it? What is it, I mean, in human life, and in the thing for the sake of which *all Scripture was given by inspiration of God?*

I will tell of three *narrow places* in human life, where God cannot be evaded.

1. And the first of these is suffering. I am well aware that I stand before a Congregation exceptionally circumstanced. A large proportion of that audience which I would ever

in this place keep prominently, predominantly in my view, might say, with an emphasis scarce elsewhere to be rivalled, *The lot is fallen unto me in a fair ground; yea, I have a goodly heritage.* It is not here that a Sermon upon affliction would be the most suitable, though we forget not how early may be the visit of pain to the life most favoured, or how keen oftentimes are the sorrows of that age to which of necessity they come as strangers.

There is no one here present who has not had some foretaste of suffering. I ask you to recall that moment of pain, mental or bodily—that one day or one hour of sharp torture, whether it was an agonized nerve of the body, or whether it was an accusing pang of conscience, or whether it was the funeral of a parent or sister, or whether it was the unutterable fear of the doom of a lost soul—recall it, I say, for one instant, in order to answer this question, Was it not the characteristic of that suffering to make you real—to unmask every lie in which you had been walking, and to say to you, Two words are true—God, and the soul? This is why we make suffering one of the three *narrow places* out of which there is no side-turning—in which, hand to hand, the battle of existence must be fought out.

The suffering of one man is no suffering to another. The loss of a dog or a bird may be anguish to one. The loss of father or brother may be no anguish to another. But all have some vulnerable part—a "heel" at which the poisoned dart may find entrance—and it is of this that I speak, whatever it be for you, when I speak of God meeting a man in suffering.

A great writer has beautifully drawn out the Mystery of Suffering in its bearing upon Conversion and the Christian Life. What would sin become without suffering? Imagine a world in which no barrier, no dyke or dam were opposed to the full-flowing river, to the ocean spring-tide, of vice and corruption. Suffering is that obstacle. You cannot sin beyond a certain point—and what that point is you cannot foresee—without some penalty or some retribution.

To one man the narrow place where the drawn sword meets him is the terrible trial of disappointment. Early, perhaps, in his educational career he was marked out as the one man for honour. Every voice gave him by anticipation the chief prize and the foremost place. He suffered no presumptuous confidence to make him idle; every faculty was exerted, every sacrifice was made, the day of hope dawned—a sudden illness barred him from the race, or an unforeseen rival stepped in and took his crown. Such experiences stop not with youth. An illustrious advocate, whose fame was equal at the Bar and in Parliament, was cut off by pining sickness just as his hand was upon the great "bauble:" he, and not he only in that Profession, had to learn that the *Most High ruleth in the kingdom of men; He putteth down one, and He setteth up another.*

To another a yet sharper stab is needed to make him feel. The narrow place for him is dishonour. Above all things that man dreaded the finger of scorn. He thought himself safe from it—so high was he in universal repute, so carefully had he stopped up each hole and each cranny of discovery. In secret he sinned, and in secrecy he trusted. The will was weak till at last it was wicked: one thing only kept in check the maturity of his wrong doing— not the fear of God, but the fear of the world. Then, if he will have it so, that shall be his suffering. In that *narrow place* God must meet with him, and the very beast which he bestrides shall fall under him with terror. Happy if in that darkest hour he shall recognize the true character of the antagonism of God—how that it is not more compelled by sin than motived by love.

To another, cast in a finer nobler mould, there is no suffering like that which is spiritual. He has played too long with scepticism. He has felt anxiously and sensitively the difficulties of believing. He has postponed decision. He has never discarded, but he has never substantiated, his Christianity. It has sufficed for him, in the sunshine of ease and prosperity, to go with the multitude, to pray shallow prayers, and to utter unmeaning praise. But now he wants it all. Something has brought it to issue. Is it true? Will it bear his weight? Can he live by it? Can he die by it? Still more urgently, Can he be holy by it? Will a prayer be heard, uttered on the strength of it? There is no turning aside, to right or left, from this one awful question; and no suffering, on this earth, is comparable in intensity to its decision. Happy he who in that cloudy and dark day, shall discern the Person of his Adversary; shall see in Him the God of Love, come to convince, to convert, to save.

2. But I cannot, in this congregation, pretend to be unaware that the *narrow place* in which God constrains the decision of His creatures concerning Himself is most often the indeed fiery trial which we call temptation.

There are men, I suppose, who pass through this life ignorant of any temptation but that negative, colourless, unimpassioned thing, which bids them, to-day, and again to-morrow, to be indolent, languid, and worldly-minded. But without disregarding such tendencies as if they were matters of indifference to the everlasting state, we would think rather, at this moment, of another and surely a larger class of our fellow-men, to whom temptation comes in a shape distinct and unmistakable, a hand-to-hand battle, and an instant, perceptible, defeat or victory.

We have known men of business, trusted with the property of a multitude of defenceless families, to whom the question has come suddenly, and must be answered on the instant, between an honesty immediately ruinous to themselves and a dishonesty eventually destructive to thousands. We are not unaware of the plausibilities by which the latter course may excuse itself; plausibilities of vague hope and fortunate accident which might make fraud advantageous and frankness calamitous. We would not be hard upon those who have found themselves unequal to such an emergency, and have been visited with a retribution upon which none can gaze with stoicism. Only we say that such an alternative was exactly one of those *narrow places* where God meets a man, to constrain him to a decision between sin and duty. It is enough to give seriousness to the life we live and to the very world we dwell in, to know that such issues are daily decided, publicly or in secret, with results so wide and so important for good or evil.

But that which happens once in a lifetime to a few, is in substance the oft-recurring trial, through forty or fifty or sixty years, of a vast multitude of men such as we are. We are all prone to sin, and the question, to sin or not to sin, is presented to us, day by day and night by night, in forms perfectly definite, and of which memory may suggest to us a thousand examples. We love to slur over the mental process by which we pass to the commission. But, as it is true that no temptation takes us but such as is common to man, so also it is true that with every temptation God, if we will look to Him, makes a way of escape. If we sin, we sin thus far deliberately, that we have an alternative proposed to us, and that we choose the wrong. In every temptation God presents Himself, and there is no evading the question between sin and obedience. Pray that our eyes may be opened, in that anxious, that brief moment, within which the will passes to the one conclusion or the other—often with the full consciousness that it is weighing and judging—to see the Divine Adversary, whose enemy in reality is the sin not the sinner, and to pray Him on the instant to guide our decision, making us then and there victorious through Him that loved us.

3. There remains yet one *narrow place* in which we must all meet God. The hour of Death.

The experiences of the past week have made very real to us the parable of that *narrowness* from which neither to the right nor to the left is any way open. Those five men imprisoned for nine days in that dark subterranean chamber of which the giant forces of earth, air and water held and kept the key—what were they but examples, in very deed, of a helplessness, of an impotency, which must one day be our own, whensoever, and by whatsoever instrumentality, it shall please God to bring us, one by one, to the last end of this wonderful, this mysterious state of being?

We speak very ignorantly of that untried future, and the fewest words concerning it may be the wisest. But, as many of us have been called, in the course of God's Providence, to stand on its threshold, in some sorrowful parting, or even in an approach of our own to the actual experience; so we must all within a few years taste death for ourselves, and ought not to do so without many previous endeavours to grasp those thoughts of it which are profitable for the living.

A narrow place, where was no way to turn either to the right hand or to the left.

Very new to the strong man, very repugnant to the nature of any man, must be that compulsion, that passivity, that involuntariness, to which the text points. To have, for the first time, *no way to turn*—neither exercise of choice, nor application of remedy, nor appeal to help; to know for ourselves the force of our Lord's saying to St Peter, *Another shall gird thee, and carry thee whither thou wouldest not;* to be unable to command one moment either to do one thing left undone, or to cancel by act or entreaty one single thing done, through all this life-time; to be compelled to go, quite alone, into a world of which we know next to nothing, with only God, long disobeyed and dishonoured and sinned against, to look to and to trust in; this must be formidable when it comes close to us, however we may put it aside or sleep over it in the dim distance.

But there is one thing which all say who have had to do with deathbeds—with any deathbeds, I mean, which are not utterly (as some are) stolid and stupid—and that is, that the look of a sin is quite different to the dying from that which it wore for the living; that the reality of it, and the freshness of it, and the wickedness of it, and the terror of it—and the way in which distances of time and space are annihilated, and the thing itself is seen, just as it was done, multiplied by a thousand doings, and magnified by a thousand aggravations never dreamed of in life—is something inconceivable without experience, something which burns itself into the very soul of that loving pity which is absolutely incapable of lightening or mitigating. *A narrow place, where was no room to turn to the right hand or to the left.*

A cry once reached me from a very young man's deathbed—and I would to God that I could make it audible to-day in some listening ear, as it never can perish again from my own— *If a man sins again and again—and then prays again and again—and then sins again and again—what can happen?*

Let us ponder that question—so characteristic of the *narrow place*, and the no exit and no turning, which has been our subject. Let us trifle no longer with that last end, nor with the journey which leads to it. Let us see that the life and the death be of one piece and one colour—faith in Christ washing white the one, faith in Christ making bright the other. *Blessed are they that have here washed their robes, that there they may have right to the tree of life.*

IV.

INDIVIDUAL INDEPENDENCE A COROLLARY OF REDEMPTION.

IV.

INDIVIDUAL INDEPENDENCE A COROLLARY OF REDEMPTION.

1 CORINTHIANS vii. 23.

Ye are bought with a price: be not ye the servants of men.

CHRISTIAN character is a Christian evidence. We all feel it so in the present. For one man who is made a Christian by argument, a thousand men have been made Christians by what St Peter calls *conversation without word;* conduct, that is, observed, felt, interpreted, without any direct preaching, or any express reference to the proofs or precepts of the Gospel. A Christian mother, a Christian wife, a Christian daughter, has been the Evangelist of many a sceptical mind, of many a careless life. It may be, with some who listen to-day, that every obstacle to infidelity has been surmounted but one, and that one is the bright example, the sweet influence, the beautiful life, of a dear person left at home yesterday, without whom immortality would not be heaven, yet with whom he who would spend eternity must spend it in the presence of Jesus Christ.

It is not only contemporaneous character which thus turns for a testimony. There is one person, laid on sleep eighteen hundred years ago, who is still a puzzle and a difficulty for the sceptic. His writings are still in our possession, as surely authenticated as any Commentaries of Cæsar or any letters of Cicero. They tell us what he was and what he became; how he began as an enemy, and how he was changed into a disciple; what was the Christianity which surrounded him, what was the faith and the life of the Church which he entered and of the Churches which he planted, what were the thoughts and the hopes which bore him up under toils and trials and temptations innumerable, in the experience of isolation, disappointment, and imprisonment, in the suspense of an ambiguous event, on the very eve of a violent death.

St Paul's witness for Christ can only be neutralized by one hypothesis. It is the hypothesis adopted by Festus—*Paul, thou art beside thyself.* "Has it ever struck you," said a most unwilling sceptic of to-day, "that St Paul was mad?" Yes, it struck Festus, it has struck many Festuses of this generation, that that busy brain had overwrought itself, that excitement had done its unsettling, its upsetting, work upon a constitution feeble perhaps originally in body, and liable, like that of most thinkers and writers, to disturbing and disarranging influences in the province of the intellect. St Paul was an enthusiast, and an enthusiast is a visionary, and a visionary is next door (at least) to a madman—there we have the key to that history, that *whirlwind out of the north,* that *great cloud,* that *fire infolding itself,* to use for a moment Ezekiel's imagery, which has had so many influences and so many consequences in the world of the Church and in the world of mankind.

When I am staggered for a moment by an explanation, which yet I feel to be no explanation, of the phenomena to be accounted for, I open the volume of St Paul's Epistles at some place like this 7th Chapter of his letter from Ephesus to Corinth, and I ask myself, Is this the visionary, is this the fanatic, is this the madman, whose inquisition is proceeding? Do I read in this Chapter the *indicia* of insanity? in this calm, level, well-balanced discussion of a perfectly matter-of-fact subject, the subject, namely, of mixed marriages between heathens and Christians, and what is to be done, under the circumstances, for the best interests of the individuals concerned, of Christianity, of society, of humanity itself? Let us imagine the reference of this question to a mind really disordered. What could be more plausible than to say, 'The entrance of the new faith into a family must of course pass the sponge over pre-existing relationships. Man and wife cannot live together if one is to sit at meat in an idol temple, and the other is to go out before day (like the Bithynian Christians of Pliny and Trajan) to "sing a hymn to Christ as God" and to bind himself by a "sacrament" to be altogether holy. Whatever the unbelieving partner may wish or urge, the Christian at all events can have no choice and no hesitation. Regardless of consequences to spouse or children, he, or she, must go forth from that dwelling, on pain of perdition, shaking off the very dust from the feet.' I can scarcely doubt that this would have been the language of some advisers; nothing, I believe, but the express direction of St Paul in this chapter keeps it from being the language of some advisers now, even as between Christian and Christian, as between the more and the less worldly, as between the more and the less devout, of two persons, both baptized and both worshipping. Or, if to stay, yet under protest, and as a compromise, and with conditions laid down, or with a perpetual look of ten thousand disapprovals. It needed great judgment, the exercise of unusual discretion, the establishment and application of very difficult principles—and in this instance without any direct aid (as he says himself) from revelation or inspiration—to lay down those great rules which he who runs may read in this chapter. If the unbelieving will go, he must go, but he shall be the one to go; the Christian shall stay if he can stay: think of the children, *sanctified* (as St Paul writes) in the one parent believing; think of the husband, think of the wife, as the case may be, who might have been saved (*how knowest thou?*) by thy staying, whom thou prejudgest, foredoomest, by thy going.

In the paragraph immediately before us St Paul has passed from primary to secondary relationships, from the domestic to the social, from questions springing out of marriage to a question springing out of slavery.

Here also I cannot but think that we have before us the workings of a remarkably sound and sensible mind.

In how many hands would Christianity have become, in those first days, a revolutionary principle. "Christian master, emancipate," "Christian slave, escape," this would have been the language of many modern Evangelists if they could be relegated into the age when slavery was an institution.

And it is perfectly true that slavery, which is, the ownership, vested in one man, of the will and action of another man, is an anti-Christian, because an inhuman, institution; and

Christianity will wage war with it, will at any cost put it down, wheresoever it has free course, whensoever it has had time to make its voice heard and its reasoning listened to. But this influence of the Gospel would be mischievous unless it were gradual. The action of Christianity is, first and above all, a spiritual action: it regenerates before it reforms: individual hearts first transformed, then social fashions are ripe for transfiguration.

Meanwhile the Gospel has a work to do, which can be done everywhere and on the instant. It can bring into every relation, whether defensible in theory or indefensible, yet at least for the present existing, a reconciling, a harmonizing, a softening and an ennobling power. It can even say, as St Paul says here, *Art thou called being a slave? care not for it. He that is called in the Lord, being a slave, is the Lord's freedman. All are bought with a price—let every man, wherein he is called, therein abide with God.*

There is one clause in this context capable of two meanings, and carrying some ambiguity, consequently, into the interpretation of the text.

Art thou called being a slave? care not for it. The Gospel makes even slavery honourable; there is an emancipation of the spirit, which no thraldom can fetter. So far we follow him.

But does St Paul go on to say, as some read him, *Nay, even if thou canst be made free, use slavery rather?* This, we feel, would be an exaggeration, rhetorical or sentimental, of which St Paul was incapable. This would just make the difference between sobriety and excitement, between religion and fanaticism, between truth and falsehood. St Paul, be quite sure, would not counsel the slave to refuse liberty if he had the choice. Though the argument carries him to the very verge of this, he knows how to stop short of it. He can say, If you are a slave, born so or made so, care not for it; even in your chains Christ has made you free. But he will not say, Slavery is better than freedom: if freedom is offered, decline it. He will not say it, and he does not. In a sentence otherwise ambiguous, there is a tense which decides. The imperative before us is the imperative of action, not of duration.

Use it rather. Use *which* rather—the old slavery, or the offered freedom? The Greek, the Greek of St Paul and the Greek of the scholar, fixes the meaning. The *use* before us is the momentary not the continuous using. *Art thou called being a slave? care not for it; yet, if thou canst*[1] *be made free, avail thyself of the chance by preference.* The same calmness, the same balance, which marks St Paul everywhere, marks St Paul here. The Paul of Festus, the Paul *beside himself*, would have gone on to

[1] The καί must be read as emphasizing the δύνασαι.

say, Slavery is better, more humbling in itself, more instructive by its contrast. The Paul of Scripture, the Paul *at the feet of Jesus,* the Paul of history and literature and world-wide influence, says, Slavery if it must be, liberty if it can; Christ's freedman anyhow, man's too if it may be. *Ye are bought with a price: be not ye,* if the choice is given you, *be not ye,* even in name, *slaves of men.*

But St Paul's words here before us have a scope much beyond this.

Even in reference to the first subject they mean more than this.

They say, In your estimates of conditions of life, in your ideas of bond and free, be not slaves of words or of men's opinion. Learn a higher lesson. See yourselves in the light of spirit, of reality, of eternity, of heaven. Reckon, not as man reckons, but as God reckons, even in things which might seem to be all of earth, all of time. The Christian slave is Christ's freedman; the Christian freeman is Christ's slave. We have a new nomenclature, we Christians; we unname and we rename all things.

Thus read, the text has indeed a lesson for all of us.

First of all, it sets in a very strong light that event, that fact, that transaction, call it what you will, which we speak of in the General Thanksgiving, of which we have just made mention in the Bidding Prayer, as *the redemption of the world by our Lord Jesus Christ.*

St Paul makes it the basis of our life. *Ye were bought for a price.* When Jesus Christ shed His blood on Calvary, He was paying a price, He was purchasing a possession. There were human instrumentalities, we know, engaged in that issue; Pharisees, Sadducees, Herodians—Judas, Caiaphas, Pilate. There were also words and acts leading up to it; a ministry exercised for three years on a footing of independence, almost of defiance; irritating, exasperating, challenging, to constituted and self-constituted authorities; works of mercy, utterances of wisdom, claims of dominion, alike offensive to the received ideas, to the popular prejudices, to the religious principles, of the time and of the race. So that, in a sense, the culminating point was reached in the way of natural cause and effect. The Crucifixion was an execution: it was the putting away of a troublesome Person, it was the closing of a vexatious struggle, it was the defeat of a formidable Antagonist, it was the reassertion of outraged rights. The will of the Sufferer was not consulted, was not expressed, at the moment of the death. *He was crucified*, St Paul himself writes, *through weakness*. Yes, and the very glory of the Sacrifice was that *weakness;* that utter self-abandonment and self-emptying; that *not clinging*, as St

Paul elsewhere writes, to the Divine *form*, to the Divine *equality*, but the taking, and the bearing, whatever it might lead to, of the nature of a servant, of the likeness of men.

Yet in that absolute self-surrender, in that suffering to be carried out, without interference and without gainsaying, the human resentments and the human passions and the human cruelties, of which the death on Calvary was, in one sense, the natural result, Jesus Christ was, in reality, making a purchase; He was buying back a self-lost, a sin-ruined world. All generations, all individuals of mankind were contained in that purchase. *Ye*, St Paul writes—people of another land and another continent, Corinthians and Europeans of a quarter of a century after the Crucifixion—ye, and if ye, then all men everywhere and for ever—*were bought for a price.* We scarcely need St Peter to interpret, *Ye were not redeemed with corruptible things, silver or gold...but with the precious blood of Christ.*

Then, if this be so, St Paul says, first, *Ye are not your own.* That is one aspect of Redemption. Then, if this be so, St Paul says again, *Be not ye*—for it would be a fraud and a dishonesty, it would be the giving away of that which is not yours to give—*be not ye slaves of men.* That is the other aspect. It is the one before us in the text.

Brethren! the task of inference and enforcement would be an easy one, were we but sure of all hearts going along with us in the premise, *Ye were bought with a price.* O, if this were the life's principle of each one; if this were the maxim engraven upon the door, the motto hung above the bed, of every young man in this audience—BOUGHT WITH A PRICE—how simple would be the duty, how prompt would be the obedience, how needless would be the preacher's office, there being what the Bible calls *such a heart* in each one. Let us think of one or two directions in which St Paul's words would guide us.

Christ's, not man's—such is the Christian. Not his own, to keep or to give away—such is that littleness which is also greatness. Such is that submission which is independence too. Such is that one service which is perfected freedom. To belong to Jesus Christ is to be a man to all else; yea, rightly interpreted, to be a man to Him.

I need not stay to guard against abuses of this saying. I need not stay to caution any one against that idea of independence, which would cut up by the roots subordination, respect, reverence, discipline, education itself. No one seriously thinks that St Paul, or St Paul's Master, is against any one of these. We must look elsewhere for the thing inculcated and the thing forbidden.

1. And first it appears to me that St

Paul's words, *Be not ye slaves of men*, have an important bearing upon the exercise of the *understanding*. *Bought with a price* by One who claims not one part but the whole of you—not more the conduct than the will, not more the energies than the affections, not more the soul (as men speak) than the reason—it cannot be safe, it cannot be right, it cannot be honest, to resign into another's keeping the exercise of the intellect upon matters of evidence or matters of doctrine; to make one man's "view," or one man's thought, or one man's faith, serve for ten or twenty or a hundred others; to attach yourself to a school or a party or a system, in such sense that you yourself shall be absolved from the task of *proving all things* as a necessary preliminary to the other duty of *holding fast* that which not others but you yourself have found to be *good*.

We are not ignorant, indeed, that an opposite course has much to recommend it. A young Clergyman, a young theologian, may speak plausibly when he says, 'I am ignorant, I am foolish, I am a child in these matters; let me follow more learned, wiser, holier men. I cannot greatly err, if I err in such company: their society, their Church, their heaven, will suffice me: at all events, it is better to go astray with such men, than to be absolutely and altogether at sea alone.'

It is thus that the ranks of Party are swollen, and the independence of our Christian Churchmanship is sacrificed. If there is humility in such language, there is also indolence, there is also impatience, there is also audacity. For is it not a bold venture, which, disparaging the Creator's apportionment to me, in whatever measure, of His gifts of reason and judgment, chooses another person, whose gifts, being ampler, shall, not assist, not supplement, but overwhelm and supersede and swallow up mine? You know, or you ought to know, that there are good men on both sides, on all sides, of everything: you, deliberately or casually, make yourself over to the good men of one. Is opinion, then, is doctrine, so immaterial, so indifferent, to the soul's health, that you can thus fling it about, thus consign it, thus put it into commission, with a light heart? Have you any right in this matter, to do what you will with that which is not your own? *Bought with a price,* every part of you, have you any right thus to make yourselves servants of men?

You fear, perhaps, the reproach, from within or from without, of having a divided mind, a suspended judgment. It is humiliating not to have your "views;" it is unfair upon others that they know not what to call you. Brethren, I know but of one thing which presses. There is one question which cannot wait—*What think ye of Christ?* Till that question is answered, the ownership hangs in doubt: *Whose am I? To whom shall I go?* But when the purchase is realized, there may be rest even in doubting. To doubt about Christ is one thing: to doubt in Christ is another thing. To doubt in Christ, a man must already have believed. To wait upon Him for light, is already, in the best sense, to have seen light. Faith is a life—till we have it, we cannot set out. Till we believe, we cannot enquire—we have none to interrogate or to listen to. But the faith which is indispensable is faith in a person: about things we may doubt and yet live. Many men must live and die in suspense—seeing the good, seeing the true, seeing the beautiful, in two opposites—unable to strike the balance, or to say in so many words, almost about anything, That is the truth. Yet the True One, the personal Truth, may be theirs all the time. Having Him, they cannot walk in darkness. Ill were such suspense, such doubting, exchanged for the most confident vaunt of partisanship—I am of Paul, or I of Apollos, or I of Cephas—yes, or I of Christ.

I know it is lonely—few men know it better —to be thus, indeed and in truth, a man of no school and no party. To have none to cheer or to echo my sayings, to have none to say of me, 'He is a good man, a sound man, one of us;' to have to listen for truth everywhere, and to gather it out of all corners; never to be able to say, 'There, I have got it all—I have builded my house, I have hewn out its seven pillars— admire its neat structure, its fair proportions' —it is not the life of ease. Let it drive me nearer to Him whose I am. He can both whisper to me one by one His secrets, and also give me strength as my day.

2. That which is true of the understanding is true also of the *conscience.*

The dispensation of the fulness of times, the Gospel of our Divine Lord, marvellous in all else, is most wonderful in this, that it offers to the individual man a direct personal contact with a revealed personal God. *I will pour out my Spirit upon all flesh…sons and daughters shall prophesy…young men and old men shall alike see visions of God…the very servants and bondwomen shall become temples of God's Spirit.* No longer shall there be a privileged order, whether of Priests or of Prophets, intervening and mediating between God and the Church, carrying His messages and reporting their replies. *I will dwell in them and walk in them …I will be their God, and they shall be my people.*

Fear not, brethren, any forgetfulness or any disparagement, from this place, of those ministerial offices which commissioned men still bear in the Church of Jesus Christ. The same Apostle who asserts most boldly the equality of all souls in the aspect of redemption and in the aspect of sanctification is above other Apostles the champion of Ecclesiastical order, and even makes this the summary of the Pentecostal gift, *He gave some to be Apostles, and some Prophets, and some Evangelists, and some Pastors and Teachers.* The work of the ministry, the edifying of the body, is carried on in the Gospel Church by ordained and commissioned men.

Nevertheless—we will say it with all boldness, as those who are bound to speak that which they deeply feel—nevertheless, there is a sanctuary within each one of us into which no minister and no brother can enter without presumption and without profanation. It is the conscience of the man in the sight of God; it is that spirit of the man which no one knoweth but the man; it is the secret shrine of motive and will, of memory and responsibility and of the life's life. It may be instructed, it may be informed, it may be influenced, it may be moved; but in every aspect save one it is free. No dictation and no direction can intrude within its precincts; for One is its Master, even Christ; and all else, even the Ministers of Jesus Christ, are here not lords but brethren. To establish over the individual conscience a right of inspection, or a right of discipline; to lay down rules for its habitual or periodical self-disclosure; to say, Without this there is no safeguard for the life, and no security for the death; this is to deny or to obscure the great characteristic of the Gospel; this is to speak a word against the all-sufficiency of the Holy Ghost as the Light and the Guide, the Remembrancer and the Comforter, of Christ's people.

Not one word shall be spoken in the tone of vulgar obloquy or vile suspicion, as regards either the motives or the manuals of such as would bring back human confession into the practice or into the preaching of the Church of England. It is not with the details, of fact or of possibility; it is not with the modes, of enquiry or of examination; it is with the idea, it is with the principle, that we have to deal, when we apply to this subject the warning voice of the text, *Bought, each and all, with a price, make not yourselves servants of men.*

We understand something of the arguments, of the reasons, for a Confessional. It has much, very much, to say for itself. We are not ignorant of the perils of an unexplored conscience. We can feel for the ignorances, for the indolences, for the procrastinations of self-judgment and self-discipline, which make havoc of so many young lives, and which almost bid us say, Better any treatment than this terrible letting alone. We sympathize with the honest effort, at no small cost of trouble, at no small sacrifice of inclination, to help towards a pure heart and a clean life those who may perhaps fear the scrutiny of man more than they fear the intuition of God, and be roused to repentance and reformation by the help of motives, powerful at least, if inferior.

Yes, if we might regard things only on the human side, as good ideas, useful inventions, powerful instrumentalities, and the like, we should be strongly tempted to accept the institution of the Confessional, or we might accept the doctrine of Purgatory, and think that we had done something to mitigate difficulties or to eke out Scripture. If we looked only at the greatness of the disease, at the difficulty of the cure, we might be disposed to advise any endeavour, however little we might feel it to be sanctioned or authorized from on high. But when we reflect upon it again and again, when we carry the matter to the Bible, when we feel the stress laid upon two things there, the individual freedom and the individual grace, when we think too how easily men may lose the muscle and sinew of their own being by having perpetual recourse to the lifting and the carrying of external assistance, we seem to come back, with a sense of relief and of satisfaction, to the suggestions of our own Church of England, which says, If you are in trouble and cannot find comfort; if you have postponed or intermitted Communion because of some weight lying upon your life; or if in the approach of death you feel something burdening your soul, and are afraid lest you should be about to stand before God with a lie in your right hand; then ask the human help of one whose office it is to guide, whose experience it is to sympathize: open your grief to him, receive his counsel; and then, if you feel that it would be comforting to have the promise brought home, to have the "ye" of the universal turned for once into the "thou" of the particular, ask him to stand over you and speak to you personally the reassuring word, *Son, be of good cheer: thy sins are forgiven thee.*

At common times, under usual circumstances, the Church's Directory is the Pulpit, and the Church's Confessional is the Congregation. There, where the bow is drawn of necessity at a venture, the arrow flies to its mark, the more felt because unseen. There, when the prayer of the preacher and the prayer of the hearer have jointly invoked the guidance which is Omniscient Wisdom, the *voice behind* will be heard again and again, saying in each emergency of the spiritual being, *This is the way, walk thou in it.* There too, in that privacy of publicity, which is the special privilege of *the Church gathered in one place*, the heart's knowledge of its own sin and its own sorrow will clothe a Liturgy, come down from past ages, with a meaning fresh and lively and powerful; will send up, from the one worshipper, a special and specific utterance to the throne of grace, and receive back into itself an answer of peace in which there shall be no "if" and no peradventure.

Independence of all save God is the prerogative of the conscience. Not in pride, but in deep self-knowledge; knowledge of the difficulty of telling into any human ear the very thing itself that is; knowledge of the perils of spiritual intimacy, alike on the one side and on the other; knowledge of the facility with which an indolent will may pass from seeking help to trusting in man; knowledge, finally, of the infinite strength which comes into us by being quite absolutely alone with God in our confidences and in our struggles; we shall feel, the weakest of us with the strongest, that, on the whole, and with a view to the eternal future, we are best as we are, without confessor and without director save in the Father and the Son and the Spirit, one God blessed for ever: we shall come back to the text, and think that it has a voice for us in this thing, *Ye were bought, each and all, with a price—be not ye servants of men.*

3. In such matters we may speak with diffidence, aware that another, even in the Church of Christ, might speak differently. But in one closing matter all will go with me: it is when I turn myself to the recollection of the *life*, and say concerning *it*, to a congregation of responsible dying men, *Bought with a price, be no man's slave.*

Naturally we are all slaves, the bravest of us and the most confident. Who has not heard and talked of the tyranny of fashion? how the manners and customs of the world lord it over us, till we are indeed *not our own;* creatures and drudges of an impersonal fugitive something, which is a power outside us not making for righteousness.

Even inside homes, with other presences powerfully influencing, we feel this, all of us. And in matters indifferent, if such indeed there are, we do well to follow it. To be singular, in regions not moral, not involving duty, is at once a waste of power, and a lack of sense. We are right, in non-essentials, in mere externals, to do even as others.

But here, brethren, in this strange yet noble life of a great English University, this tyrant fashion bears with crushing weight upon all of us. Sometimes it assails us in the more open forms of laxity of speech or action, of jesting with things sacred, of making light of morality, of making a mock at sin. Sometimes it bids us possess ourselves of that which we cannot pay for—*Every one has it, Every one does so*—regardless of the many self-denials which made it possible for us to be here, of the many prayers which followed us, of the many tears which will fall over our misdoing. Sometimes it simply bids us trifle; takes a trivial estimate of work, of a career, of the future; bids us neglect instruction, postpone reading, leave everything serious to the chance and to the accident.

And in all this we think ourselves free! doubly free—free even from the thing that is right—even from religion—even from duty!

Free? St Paul calls us slaves—slaves of men, slaves one of another—of the meanest of us, and the poorest, and the vilest. *Rejoice, O young man, in thy youth: walk in the sight of thine eyes, walk in the way of thy heart: but know thou that for all these things God will bring thee*—not thy brother, not fashion, not the world, but thee, thine own self—*into judgment.*

Therefore it is that I have chosen for you to-day the text, *Bought with a price—be not slaves.*

Bought with a price. Christ bargained for thee, bid for thee, tried and toiled for thee, died, shed His very blood for thee. Let not the scoffer rob thee of that word: thou wilt want it one day.

O, if, when you lie down and when you rise

up—if, when you go forth to the Chapel or to the Lecture-room—if, when you refresh and when you amuse yourselves, in ways which need not be wicked, which only become so when you forget God in them—you would just say to yourselves that word, *I was bought with a price*, Jesus Christ died for me, Jesus Christ shed His precious blood for me—you do not know what a charm there would be in it. Toil rest, recreation blessing, the common holy, earth heaven—try it, try it for a day! Say to yourself, There was One who cared for me, had me in His view ages before I was born; there is One now who looks upon me with love, such love as is not on this earth, so tender, so strong, so living; and He actually paid a price for me, for me, so worthless, so nothing. Yes, if you would do this, you know not what a joy, what a sweetness, would enter into your life. You would not care then, by comparison, what others thought: it would be enough to know this, that, working or resting, alone or in company, joyous or sorrowful, living or dying, you are His. He has thought you worth paying for—which is to say, worth dying for. Shall it be too much to ask of you, that you would just accept that love, just cherish it, just live it, just hand it on?

Bought with a price, be not slaves of men. Look not upon their present smile or frown. Let them not own you. They never died for you. Let them not turn and twist you whither they will. Be a man—human, humane, manly, manful—which is to say, *a Christian.*

O noble independence! the liberty of the man that is God's, and that has God in him: the liberty which is only not licence: the liberty of the son who abides in the house for ever, not of the slave who has no inheritance in the Home and no permanence.

V.

ONE THING THOU LACKEST.

V.

ONE THING THOU LACKEST.

MARK x. 21.

Then Jesus beholding him loved him, and said unto him, One thing thou lackest.

THIS paragraph of the Gospels is a striking example of that harmony in variety which unfriendly critics love to exaggerate into discrepancy.

Three of the Evangelists have preserved the incident. Each one adds something to the completeness of the picture. The wealth of the enquirer is brought into view by all of them; but St Matthew alone tells us that he was young, and St Luke alone speaks of him as a ruler, while St Mark gives several most interesting particulars of the interview itself— the running and the kneeling, the earnestness and the reverence, and the look which Christ gave him, and the love which Christ felt for him; and then again the look which Christ threw upon the disciples as He drew the moral, and the repeated expressions of astonishment with which they received His unexpected words as to the spiritual dangers of worldly wealth. All this variety, so picturesque and so natural, would be ill exchanged, we all feel, for a dry and sterile uniformity of narrative, taking out of it all the life and all the play, and suggesting the idea of an inspiration merely mechanical, out of which the human element would have departed, and with it (rightly understood) also the Divine.

There is, however, in this instance, amongst many variations which are entirely and beautifully harmonious, just one which might appear at first sight to be of a different character.

St Mark and St Luke give thus the question and counter-question with which the conversation opens. *Good Master, what shall I do that I may inherit eternal life?* Jesus said, *Why callest thou me good? There is none good but one, that is, God.* St Matthew, according to the best Manuscripts, expressly confirmed by the testimony of Origen early in the third century, prior therefore to any of our existing Manuscripts of the Greek Testament, gives the two clauses a very different form. According to him the question was, *Master, what good thing shall I do, that I may have eternal life?* and the answer, *Why askest thou me about that which is good? there is but One that is good;* as though He would correct the enquiry about a particular good thing to be done in order to win heaven, by recalling the questioner to the one source and spring of all good, in whom alone, sought and found and lived in, can the true *eternal life* be entered by any man.

It might be suggested that some copyist, jealous for the Saviour's honour, had substituted this reading for the common one, which seemed to disclaim for our Lord the title of *good*. It is enough to say in answer—apart from the general precariousness of such conjecturing—that no such alteration has been made by the same Manuscripts in the other two Gospels, and that Origen himself calls attention to the variety in this place between the two Evangelists and the one.

But we can all see that this is an example, when carefully looked into, not of contradiction, but (which is a widely different thing) of unexplained consistency.

St Matthew omits the word *good* before *Master*, and throws the whole weight of the reply upon the word *good* before *thing*. The other Evangelists say, *Good Master;* and *what thing,* instead of *what good thing, shall I do?* They represent the comment upon *good* in the answer as referring to the appellation of our Lord Himself in the question. Is there any thing impossible or improbable in the supposition that both accounts of the matter are true? that the question may have been (as indeed the English Version gives it in St Matthew), *Good Master, what good thing shall I do...?* and that the answer may have touched upon both the uses of *good*—*Why callest thou me good?* without knowing what thou sayest, without knowing that One only is good, and that, if I am good, it is in virtue of a Divinity which is not in thy thought? And again, Why askest thou about some particular good thing to be done to merit life, when in reality *good* is not a thing but a Person, and he who would enter into life must do so by knowing and loving and becoming like to Him?

Thus the two narratives may complete, by supplementing, each other. Each may bear its part faithfully in the preservation of the sacred whole. It is not given us, as yet, to combine the narratives certainly: enough, if we see that one combination, at least, is possible; nay, if we did not see it, we could trust the Word of God still.

Who cannot feel, in this instance, the truthfulness, the importance, of each form of the saying?

When Christ says, *Why callest thou me good?* He certainly does not mean to accuse Himself of sin. On proper occasions He could boldly face His enemies with the question, *Which of you convicteth me?* Nor does He deny here that Divinity which lies at the root of all His sayings, as much in the first three Gospels as in the fourth; as much in *The Son of Man shall send forth His Angels,* or *No man knoweth the Son but the Father,* or *Lo, I am with you alway,* or *All power is given unto me in heaven and in earth,* of St Matthew, as in the *I and my Father are one,* or *The glory which I had with thee before the world was,* of the sealing testimony of St John. What our Lord does correct in this questioner is the ignorant complimenting which can bestow upon one whom he regards only as a human Rabbi, as a fellow-creature therefore and a fellow-sinner with himself, a title which has its only true place as an attribute of God Himself, and therefore of One whom faith has learned to address with undoubting affiance as *My Lord and my God.* To meet this young ruler with the unexpected check, 'Ask thyself why thou callest me good; recollect what *good* means, and to whom alone it belongs?' was one part, we believe, of that discipline in thoughtfulness which his case demanded, and which is pursued with severe gentleness in the whole treatment which follows.

And then, when Christ goes on to say, 'Why askest thou me about some good act of thine which is to earn heaven? recollect, One, and but One, is good, and in Him, not in thyself or in thy little doings, is eternal life'—do we not read here the correction of a thousand mistakes and presumptions and ignorances which have survived into our own time and into our own religion? Do we not hear Him saying to us, Build not upon the sand, set not up your little towers of self-righteousness and vainglory, but go to the Fountain of Life, seek Him who is the Author of all godliness, acquaint thyself first with Him and be at peace, then come and offer thy gifts, not to win, but because thou hast won, the grace of a free salvation?

We have before us a history, a character,

a life: one which has repeated itself many times in human experience; one which may be here to-day, not in the book only, but in flesh and blood.

This young man, immortalized in the everlasting Word, was not a phenomenon, he was a type.

We see him so distinctly in his own question, *What shall I do that I may inherit eternal life?* Yes, here is enquiry—anxiety therefore, desire to be right, admission that there may be a higher height, a loftier attainment, than the life has yet reached; respect too and reverence for One who is neither Priest nor Rabbi nor Ruler, who has neither rank, nor office, nor philosophy, nor oratory, but only the two things, sincerity and sanctity, to recommend Him: this there is in the young man, and it brings him where all are welcome who would know and do; brings him running, brings him worshipping, and sets him face to face with Jesus Christ. A solemn moment —for him whose life was then in the balance, and for thousands and tens of thousands who shall read of it to the end of time.

And this spirit of enquiry, and this spirit of reverence, was no sudden or violent impulse, separate from, and at variance with, the days and years of the past. There was a third thing in that character; a memory of morality, a habit of virtue. There was nothing to call up a tell-tale blush on that countenance, if men spoke of integrity, spoke of purity, spoke (in any form) of duty. There is not a doubt thrown, throughout the narrative, upon the truth, upon the consistency, of the profession, *All these have I kept*. At the very moment that he is asking, *What shall I do?* his heart is saying within him, *What lack I yet?*

A curious mixture, we might say, an improbable combination, of humility and self-righteousness, if we had never read a heart, if we knew not our own. This youth, so earnest, so respectful, so moral, is yet a dweller in the tents of the self-man; he still dreams of improving himself into perfection; he still fancies that, if the fabric of the self-righteousness can but be raised one tier, one story, higher, its top may reach heaven—unaware that its foundation is in the sand; unaware of the great coming storm which shall mix earth and sky. *Ignorant of God's righteousness, going about to establish his own,* he has not one thought, as yet, of the *submission* (as St Paul calls it) which is the first step of life.

He thinks, perhaps, when he asks that question, *What good thing shall I do?* of some little finishing stroke, some last ornament and embellishment of perfectness, which may cost him an effort, but which at least need not undo nor unmake anything. He thinks, we might say—if the anachronism could be pardoned—of some large gift of money, to Mission or Hospital, which shall yet leave him *something;* of some pilgrimage, to shrine or sepulchre, from which yet there may be a return; of some penance, whether of infliction or of abstention, which may at least leave him living. There is almost nothing, he says to himself in the distance, which he would refuse to bear or to dare for his soul's health: there is even a desire to suffer something if he may but be perfect: name the price, he says to his new Master, and I will pay it—only tell me the secret of a certified safety, of an absolute self-satisfaction.

We might have been tempted, we scribes of the kingdom, to throw ourselves instantly, with all the weapons of an Evangelical armoury, upon the radical fault of this sort of questioning. We might have said, *I perceive that thou art yet in the gall of bitterness,* tied and bound with the fetter of a fatal Pharisaical self-deception. We might have precipitated, as a first duty, the preaching of grace, and called him to seek, *with strong crying and tears*, what St Paul bids us to describe as *justification of life*.

Very different, quite opposite to this, is the Saviour's treatment. Instead of arguing, He accepts; takes him on his own ground; bids him save himself; arrays before him the ten Commandments—nay, not the ten; just the six of the Second Table—just those in which the young man counts himself perfect; and so elicits from him the avowal of an entire self-complacency, *All these I have kept from my youth up;* and leads him to expect confidently the instant reply, 'Rich for heaven as for earth, eternal life is thine.'

We pause with the character full in view, to contemplate it for a moment with the eye of man. We confront with it two opposite schools of doctrine, and hear the one saying, 'The man is worse than a profligate;' and the other, 'The man is safe, and only wants perfecting.' The one says, Better any immorality than the vice of self-righteousness. The other says, Morality is the *differentia* of human being; give me virtue, and for all else let bigots fight. The one says, No case so hopeless as that which has *no need of repentance;* which, not having consciously fallen, can dispense with a Saviour; saying, *I am rich,* is deaf to the counsel, *Buy of me without price.* The other says, The end of religion is virtue—reach virtue any way, and God cannot condemn.

Against the former of these views is the *Jesus loved him:* against the latter is the *went away sorrowful.* It is better to be moral than to be profligate; yet to be moral is not salvation. We must not sever what the text has joined in one—

Jesus beholding him loved him, and said unto him, One thing thou lackest.

We shall not suppose, with a whole Gospel

against us, that Christ here approves, as sufficient, a legality which leaves out its own first Table; which contents itself with half the Decalogue; which is, in the first place, morality without religion, and which is, in the second place, a morality of mere negation: not to have defrauded, not to have stolen, not to have murdered, it is enough—enter thou into life, into glory.

Nor shall we force the words given us by St Matthew, *If thou wilt be perfect,* into a sense utterly unevangelical—Salvation and perfection are ideas distinct and different: *If thou wilt enter into life, keep the commandments; If thou wilt be perfect, do something besides.* According to this view, and in substance it is the view of a vast and pretentious Communion, there are, first, commandments of necessity, and there are, secondly, counsels of perfection: there are requirements for the many, and there are ambitions for the few: it is not necessary to be perfect; something less will suffice: a man may be saved with thus much, if without more he may not shine.

When Christ says to this moral young man, *Yet lackest thou one thing,* we understand Him to say, *And that one thing is needful.* He who puts it from him, as either unnecessary for him or unattainable, counts himself unworthy of everlasting life. He who refuses that one thing, and goes away sorrowful because he is not accepted without it, certainly has not failed only in some adornment or corollary of sainthood: if he does not come back for it, to Christ in flesh or to Christ in glory, assuredly he has lost himself; having his good things here, he has none to look for across death and the grave.

Yet *Jesus beholding him loved him.*

There are few words more touching in all Scripture. They mark so decisively the perfect humanity of Jesus Christ. Not one that cannot sympathize—no, but one, in all things, *of like passions with us*, only *without sin*. The holy Saviour had a *loved* one among His disciples. He did not command, He did not exemplify, a dead level, a dull monotony, even of feeling, even of affection. There was for Him a friend among the friends—one chosen among the elect—one heart with which His heart beat yet more sensitively than with other hearts all loved.

But there is more than this in the text. This young man was a stranger to Him. Apart from the Omniscience of Deity—and this is not now the thing in question—He had no knowledge of him until now. And now that He first sees him, can He altogether approve? Read together the two halves of the text, and the first becomes more wonderful by the combination—*One thing*, the one thing, he lacked; and yet Jesus, beholding him, loved him.

That look, and that love, like all else in Our Lord, were full of instruction. Do you suppose that the Blessed Lord now in heaven looks with equal love upon opposite characters amongst ourselves? say, upon the young man of pure life and clean heart and beautiful feeling, and the young man whose very soul is *a cage of unclean birds,* whose tongue is profane, unchaste, or cruel, whose conduct towards his own is selfish, unmannerly, hard, ungrateful? Ought He, we ask it with reverence, ought He so to do? Ought Jesus Christ to confound all differences even amongst those who still *lack one thing?*

Such teaching is as unscriptural as it is immoral. It would make us shut the Bible if we read it there. It would be an argument against Christianity which all the Evidences could not parry. It would be the indication of a looseness and a roughness and a coarseness of judgment, which could not be attributed without impiety to the Judge of all men. Because we believe that there is a discriminating quality—and the Gospel calls it faith—visible already, in the case of each one, as present or absent, to the eye of God; shall we go on to say that without this or apart from this there is no essential difference between vice and virtue? *Let the Judge of all the earth do right,* however it may fit in with our ideas or with our theologies. Be not rash in *fixing the great gulf*—wipe not out the *Jesus loved* in your zeal to hurry towards the *One thing thou lackest.*

What a view does this open to us of the love of Jesus Christ now for many a young man, earnest, moral, thoughtful, enquiring, whom yet He cannot excuse—cannot for his sake excuse—from the choice and the decision and the self-surrender, *Go and sell—then come and follow.* Yes, He loves, and we ought to love, the beauty of the character, the openness of the mind, the cleanness of heart and hand, the reverence of soul and spirit. He loves, and we ought to love, the appreciation of His wisdom, the recognition of His holiness, the admiration of His sacrifice, in many who cannot yet quite say to Him, *My Lord and my God*. He loves, and we ought to love, the dutiful son, the kind brother, the faithful friend, the diligent student, the bright example—the six Commandments kept from the youth up, the eagerness to know, from such as are worthy to tell, whether indeed there be a yet more excellent way into a joy and an immortality believed in. It is no sign of jealousy for Christ's honour to withhold the love He gave, or to mingle in one sweeping sentence the righteous of earth and the wicked. The blessed Lord can discriminate—even His followers should do so—between such a youth as we have sketched in these sentences, and the frivolity, the idleness, the gluttony, the immorality, which make up its opposite. The heart-searching eye pauses in its survey of the world and its fulness to distinguish and to discern. He beholds and He loves the thing that is good, even where that very love constrains Him to the further saying, *One thing thou lackest.*

One thing. Often have we said, of friend or neighbour, He has but one fault. Perfect in uprightness, in diligence, in devotion, he lacks temper, or he lacks courtesy, or he lacks charity. Perfect in kindness, in consideration, in humility, he lacks strength, or he lacks courage, or he lacks exertion. Sometimes we have to say a more serious thing. So faultless in one aspect, in one half of the man—so tender, so generous, so unselfish, so useful— he cannot quite be trusted when the question is of truth, or of sincerity, or of integrity, or of virtue. He has one fault, and it carries unsoundness into everything. We all know that there are vices which no number of virtues can counterbalance, in the judgment of the world, or in the judgment of the Christian.

Thus the saying, *One thing thou lackest*, is capable of many applications, some of them qualifying, others condemning. It depends upon the nature of the one thing. There are defects, there are blemishes, there are faults; there are also sins, and vices, and crimes.

We have touched upon the question, Which of the two was it here? And we have been compelled to understand the one want in this case as a fatal want, not in the region of conduct, but in the region of spirit; not in the region of the world's judgment, not even in the region of the moralist's judgment, but in the sight of God, in the foreview of heaven.

That which was lacking to this young man was, in one word, devotion. Not devotion in the sense of devoutness, but devotion in the sense of self-surrender. A young man who knelt down before Christ in the public highway was certainly not wanting in reverence. We can believe that, not in the spirit of ostentation but of sincere piety, he was one who prayed, many a time and oft, in the synagogues and in the streets. He was on the very verge and margin of a higher devotion still. This was his *valley of decision,* and he is gone down into it. This day he is to make that determination after which he can never be quite the same. He is asking the question of questions; that question which was life from the dead to Saul of Tarsus and to the jailor of Philippi; that question which filled the Church of Christ on the day of Pentecost, and which has been to countless thousands from that year to this the turning-point between two lives and two eternities. But in this case there is a false ring, not of hypocrisy but of self-deception, in the good words. *What shall I do—what good thing shall I do—that*

I may have eternal life? We will not be extreme to mark the word *do:* it was in Paul's question, it was in the jailor's question, it was in the question of Pentecost and the three thousand. It was only in the ear of Jesus Christ that the false ring was perceptible, and He applied to it a test at once stern and gracious.

God and Mammon are at issue in that heart. It is attempting the impossible thing, to reconcile the two services and the two ownerships: and when it says, *What shall I do?* it means, What shall I do that is compatible with being young, and rich, and a ruler; with being a man of means, and a man of the world? The question itself has a condition lying under it, and that condition gives it the lie in the very asking. Flattery would give a soft answer. Jesus Christ says, *Sell that thou hast:* fling away thy riches, part with thine all, keep nothing, strip thyself of house and land, of purse and treasure, of importance and influence, of power to give, and power to bequeath; then (if we may for the moment keep the reading) *take up the cross,* that accursed badge and implement of Roman tyranny, not yet possessing its one tender and gracious association—take it up, as one that shall die upon it, and that accepts the sentence. All is mysterious, all is repulsive, all is terrific to the hearer—one word alone lights up the darkness; one word alone blends severity with goodness—*Follow me!* Be my companion as I tread the way of homelessness and poverty, of reproach and ignominy, at last of torture, murder, martyrdom; share my reviling, desertion and repudiation by mine own; soothe with thy companionship sorrows which thou canst and sorrows which thou canst not partake in; listen day by day to my teaching, drink in my revelation of a life above and beyond this life; print my likeness upon thee, that thou mayest represent and reproduce it when I am unseen. This shall be the present recompense of the self-devotion which I ask of thee. *A thousandfold now in this time* it shall be to thee for all that thou sacrificest, riches and lands, kinsfolk and friends, honours and affections; *with*—yes, I hide it not—*with persecutions: and in the world to come,* just out of sight, just beyond death, *in the world to come*—promise above all promise—*eternal life.*

This, brethren, is the *love* of Jesus Christ—it stops not with gilding and refurbishing time, it sets open eternity. *One thing thou lackest*—thy soul must be athirst till she has it—union with the alone Good One, the having Him in thee, the being at one with Him now and world without end. To have this, thou must part with all else: in act, if Christ bids thee; in will, at all events, because Christ calls thee. Art thou equal to this? Is thy hold upon the unseen such as to detach thee from the visible?

Brethren! it is the question proposed to us in all things. It meets us when the life of the body is buoyant and jubilant, and the tempter spreads before us the pleasant excess, the luxurious wantoning, the delicious, delirious sensuality. It meets us at the great turning-points of life, when the choice must be made, of the profession, of the abode, of the companionship, of the wedlock. It meets us in the rising within us of the jest sparkling but profane, of the retort telling but cruel, of the story amusing but scandalous, of the judgment, on men or things, popular but iniquitous. *This world* or *that world* is written for us upon everything: *Rest and enjoy,* or else, *Go and sell;* have thy good things, or wait for them; drink of earth's cup, or else, *take the cross, and follow.*

Who that knows himself shall much marvel

at the result of this appeal in the case of the rich young ruler? Was it not something, that he went away *sorrowful?* Was it not something, that anger, that scorn, that fierce resentment, marked not the ruin of the hope and the disappointment of the aspiration? Might he not have said, 'Thou dost indeed know how to quench the smoking flax—thou hast indeed the art of despising, of frustrating, the day of small things? I was here ready to the hand of judicious fostering, and thou hast thrown me back into the burning from which tenderness would have plucked me?'

He went away sorrowful. The love of Jesus was wasted upon him for this time, and the Gospels which tell of the going tell of no return. The moral, at all events, is thus written. It is not the second chance, it is not the late hope, it is not the *last first,* which is here recorded for our learning: it is the peril of refusing Christ's call; of saying to Him, *I will not,* when He bids us follow; of preferring earth when He offers heaven.

Brethren! Jesus Christ has sent us once again this day the word of His grace, saying, Halt no more between two opinions. Defer not for one day the vital decision. Whatsoever it be which stands at this moment between thee and thy soul, cast it from thee. Sloth or cowardice, appetite or passion, bosom lust or besetting sin, renounce, hate, expel it, at Christ's bidding. Rise, He calleth thee; take up thy cross at once, and follow.

What would it be on the last day of life, what would it be on the morning of the judgment, to feel in the awakening conscience this conviction, *One thing I lack?* Too late to go back to fetch anything out of the house; too late to supply one want or to wash out one sin: much more to relay the foundations of the whole being, to bring into it a new spring and a new motive and a new aim of life. Who shall risk the hearing then, from the lips of the Judge, *One thing was needful, and that one thing thou lackest?* O let us enter now into that greatest, gravest of questions, *What must I do to be saved?* and may God, who has all hearts in His hand, dispose each one of us to say, and to mean the saying, *I count all things but loss, that I may win Christ.*

VI.

AN HUNDREDFOLD NOW IN THIS TIME.

VI.

AN HUNDREDFOLD NOW IN THIS TIME.

MARK x. 29, 30.

There is no man that hath left house, or brethren, or sisters, or father, or mother, or wife, or children, or lands, for my sake, and the Gospel's,

But he shall receive an hundredfold now in this time, houses, and brethren, and sisters, and mothers, and children, and lands, with persecutions; and in the world to come eternal life.

A PROMISING enquirer has just come to the Saviour; has come, and is gone again. Running, and kneeling, as one in haste to be saved, and assured of the power of Christ to save, a rich young ruler has proposed to Him the question of questions, has received a clear answer, and is gone away sorrowful. An exceptional case had required an exceptional treatment: and He who laid no such compulsion upon others of His followers, upon the Zaccheuses and Philemons and Gaiuses of the kingdom, has judged it necessary to lay the compulsion of poverty here: *Go thy way: sell whatsoever thou hast, and give to the poor; and thou shalt have treasure in heaven: and come, follow me.*

Something very beautiful there was in the character thus severely handled; for it is expressly mentioned, and in this the case stands alone, that *Jesus beholding him loved him.* Yet not the less, but all the more for this love, He dealt truly with him; saw that he was worth saving, and could only be saved thus: the world had so tight a hold upon him, that no mere self-denial, in the way of abstemiousness or almsgiving, would suffice to detach him: by one stroke the chain must be broken, the captive must be set free: if he really wished to be saved, and if he really meant what he said when he called Jesus *good*, he will bow himself to the hard necessity, and count it more than compensated by the Divine companionship of which this is the condition.

But to so lofty, so superhuman, an estimate of loss and gain this young man is not equal. He would have joyfully heard how to combine two worlds: but if one world only can be his, then it must be the world of present enjoyments; of young interests, human flatteries, and great possessions.

A reflexion upon the terrible dangers of riches is the first moral of the incident. The disciples, indeed, more experienced, some of them, in the opposite perils of poverty, with its mean toils and down-dragging cares and ready envyings, exclaim in astonishment, *Who then can be saved?* If the rich, with their tranquil days and easy fortunes, with every facility for the two virtues of honesty and of thankfulness, can *hardly enter* God's kingdom, how much less, surely, they whose whole life is trial—trial of patience, trial of rectitude, trial of faith. Thus it is that each rank and each age and each character regards its own as the very chief of all difficulties and all hindrances, thinks any other class or condition better off for salvation, and asks, in despondency, if not in recrimination, If that other, that opposite, can scarcely be saved, how, how can I?

But there was one disciple, who, in those days of his ignorance and self-reliance, was ever ready to compare himself advantageously with other men, and who saw, in the example of this young ruler going away sorrowful, an opportunity of vaunting the opposite conduct of those who, like himself, had counted all things loss for Christ. *Peter began to say to Him, Lo, we have left all, and have followed Thee.*

Our Lord begins His reply to this boast by a warm and generous recognition of the greatness and blessedness of their self-sacrifice. The tone may be faulty—self-assertion is ever unpleasing—but not on this account shall the Saviour for one moment depreciate the devotion on which He shall build His Church. There is no man who has done what ye have done, and shall not, here and hereafter, have his reward. *Now in this time an hundredfold. In the world to come eternal life.*

In the enumeration of the particulars of the hundredfold, we may notice, in passing, two omissions. They are characteristic, we think, of the Master's teaching. The one omission is that of the *father*, the other omission is that of the *wife*. The one omission may seem faintly to foreshadow the Divine rule elsewhere laid down, *Call no man your father upon the earth; for one is your Father, which is in heaven.* Fathers *an hundredfold* might have favoured the delusion of a spiritual direction, a human authority, below, such as is utterly at variance with the idea of a Dispensation in which, under the guidance of an indwelling Spirit, *all shall be*, individually and immediately, *taught of God*. The mother, like the brother and the sister, may reappear, with multiplication, in the recompense: unity is the very condition of the new, the spiritual, fatherhood; not even in name or in figure can it be departed from.

The other omission is illustrative, I venture to think, of the purity, of the delicacy, of the Saviour's teaching. He will not even seem to open to His disciples a Mahometan Paradise. Sisters a hundredfold—not so much as in parable the other.

Large and generous as is the promise, for this life and for that which is to come, love itself adds one caution to this glowing picture. The end is not yet. While earth is still earth, hope and fear are still indispensable ministers in the Church and in the heart. *Many that are first shall be last, and the last first.* Amongst the original hearers there stands a Thomas that shall doubt, a Peter that shall deny, a Judas that shall betray. A few years hence, on the other hand, there shall be a Mark that deserts in Pamphylia, yet will re-enlist himself in Antioch, and will live to be a comforter of Apostles, yea, an Evangelist of the Churches: a Saul, once (he says it of himself) a *blasphemer and a persecutor*, yet made *willing in the day of Christ's power*, and chosen out of all men to make the light of the Gospel shine throughout the world. Yes, there shall be, in this as in all things, *first last, and last first:* be not disdainful, but charitable—be not highminded, but fear.

St Matthew records at this point a whole Parable devoted to this theme. The labourer early called, early obedient, must not despise, must not envy, the later call, or the later obedience of another. God gives not account, to us, of His dealing with His own. There is a spirit of contempt and cavilling which may even forfeit the crown. *Last shall be first, and first last.* Not the start, but the arrival, is the thing in question. *He that endures to the end shall be saved.*

We have, then, before us, as the principal subject, a magnificent view of the compensations of discipleship.

Some have talked slightingly of the sacrifices made by Peter and his companions. They are supposed to have had little to give up. A crazy boat or two, a few tattered nets—this was their all. The word 'fisherman' carries to our ears, in spite of the hired servants, and the house in Capernaum, an almost inevitable impression of low rank and poor circumstances. On the other hand, it does not appear that at the time of this occurrence their abandonment of home or employment was either final or absolute. After the Resurrection the disciples are found in Galilee, resuming, at least occasionally, their old occupations.

Nevertheless they rightly regarded the call to follow Jesus as a call to give up everything for it. From that moment they belonged to Another. Whithersoever He led, they must follow. Never again would they be their own for a single hour. It was a true instinct which made Peter combine in consecutive clauses, and as equivalent phrases, the *left all* and the *followed Thee*. An entire detachment from all that had made and been the old life was the very condition and meaning of the new. To leave house and lands, brethren and sisters, father and mother, wife and children, for Christ's sake and the Gospel's, was the solemn act of self-dedication, the very sign and sacrament of discipleship, by which a new convert cut himself off from the Judaism or from the heathenism (as the case might be) in which he had heretofore lived and moved and had his being. It was just what a man of the highest caste in India has to do at this day if he can make up his mind (and no wonder if in such cases it is a rare thing) to adopt Christianity. Every commonest act of his life has been connected with the worship of an idol deity; and to tell him that you will excuse him from giving up caste, that you will allow him to be a Brahmin and yet a Christian, is something much beyond the permission to bow himself now and then in the house of Rimmon: it is a licence to combine in perpetuity the service of Christ and the service of Belial, to be an habitual partaker at once of the table of the Lord and of the table of devils. The man must leave all, if he is to follow Christ.

No doubt, when the Christian Church began to plant itself everywhere, with its congregations and communities regularly organized, so far from disturbing social order or breaking up family connexions, it tended rather to confirm and consolidate each. Every word of the Epistles implies the recognition of all existing relationships, and the continuance of every believer in the condition and circumstances in which he was called. Husbands and wives, parents and children, masters and slaves, all were to remain as Christ found them, only bringing into each duty and each relation a consecrating motive and a sanctifying principle. The Gospel came to transfigure, not to revolutionize; to remodel spiritually, not ostensibly, the various functions and institutions of society. Henceforth the literal leaving all was to be the higher effort, the more ambitious enterprise, of certain exceptional ministries. The man who amidst the refinements of a well-appointed home, or the proprieties of a nicely ordered Parish, hears within him the voice of Jesus Christ bidding him to carry the Gospel across sea and land into some region where all is still confusion and darkness, enters literally into the experience of Apostles of old, who could say, humbly and thankfully, to the Saviour who chose and sent, *Lo, we have left all and have followed Thee.* Doubtless too there are many who ought to hear this voice and will not. Doubtless, both in the choice of Professions, and in the subsequent choice of places and circumstances of service, there is still, in us all, a niceness and a fastidiousness, a self-sparing and a self-pleasing, which is effeminate, cowardly, and therefore anti-Christian. We use far too lightly the word 'impossible.' We pick and we choose far too daintily amongst alternatives presented. We refuse to count amongst the alternatives all that is rough and hard, and therefore perhaps the more Christ-like, in the answers to that enquiry which yet we all profess to open, or we could not write ourselves Christians, *What shall I do, Lord? What wilt Thou have me to do?*

There are some present in this Congregation, whose lives are not yet shaped, as to the particular calling. They cannot too soon or too seriously remember that, in this age and in this country at least, literally *the field is the world*. The possibilities of service are unbounded. Let no silly sneers, let no infidel taunts, prevail to suggest to you that the Gospel of Jesus Christ has lost its old strength and life for evangelizing, that the Mission-field is effete and sterile, or that the living Saviour has in any respect modified what have been aptly called His Church's marching orders, *Go ye into all the world—make all the nations disciples*—and then, and in so doing, *Lo, I am with you alway.*

But here, speaking from this Pulpit, and after a week so memorable in reference to this more Apostolical work, this indeed Divine life, no tone of address seems so suitable as that of intense thankfulness to the Author and Giver of every perfect gift for the grace which He has bestowed and for the prospect which He has opened. The lives which have given and are giving themselves to the Cambridge Delhi Mission are described, by those who know, as the very salt and light of our society. And yet we grudge them not to India. For we know that, in this as in all sacrifices made for Christ's sake and the Gospel's, to keep is to lose, and to give is to have. From every such self-dedication, another springs, and another, and another; life generates life, in spiritual things, as surely as death breeds death: such men bear away with them from amongst us influences which we can ill spare, but (with Elisha of old) we 'see' them as they are taken, and lo, *a double portion of their spirit* rests upon the staying.

For the rest of us, for whom it is too late to rearrange the life, or to whom it is not given to dream of magnificent sacrifices, it must suffice—and this shall not lack its blessing—to stretch after them the hands of sympathetic interest and of bountiful aid; to keep alive amongst ourselves the flame of that zeal for Gospel progress which has borne them hence in person; to see that there be no lack of offerings—head, heart, and hand—to cherish and to subsidize; so that they may never doubt, in their far-off Mission, the memory of the love of that University whose sons and whose ambassadors they are, and that there may be a continuous succession (God grant it) of devout and devoted men, to strengthen their hands living, and, as the need shall arise, to be baptized for the dead.

In comparison with such enterprises of faith and devotion, it may seem a small thing to speak of the less definite but not less real self-dedications which are certainly within our reach; the leaving all, in heart and will, for Christ's sake and the Gospel's; the marking every treasure and every possession, intellectual or material, with the true 'Corban,' which is, *Holiness to the Lord;* the so subordinating every taste and every affection as that we shall remember and not forget Him in each; the bringing every thought and every attachment into captivity (as St Paul writes) to Jesus Christ and Him crucified. Whoso does this does all: he too is a servant and an Apostle: he too hath, in spirit, *left house and land* for Jesus: he too *shall receive an hundredfold* in this life and in the life to come.

This is the discipleship. Now for its compensations. Our Lord divides them. There is a compensation in the present: *now in this time.* The nature of it is remarkable. *He shall receive an hundredfold now in this time, houses, and brethren, and sisters, and mothers, and children, and lands.* The very language shows the promise figurative. We have read it, perhaps, as quite vague. 'Shall receive something instead, something which shall reconcile him to the loss, of all these.' An inward peace, suppose—a sense of God reconciled—an appreciation of the littleness of things temporal—a growing deepening apprehension of things invisible and eternal.

Is there not something besides—something more precise, more peculiar—in this promise?

Brothers, sisters, mothers, children—an hundredfold, each and all of these, now, in this time—no mere equivalent, in the dim shadowy future, for the sacrifice of them here? Surely the speech is concerning that wonderful feature of the blessed Gospel—the brotherly, sisterly, filial, parental love (as the case may be) which is between Christians as Christians; that love which Christ Himself inaugurated, in the words which He uttered, in figure, concerning Himself, *Who is my mother, and who are my brethren? Whosoever shall do the will of God, the same is my brother, and my sister, and my mother.* It is so with His disciples. He who once makes up his mind to be Christ's entirely and in everything, must expect, must be prepared, to leave all for Him. All that was of nature, all that is of choice—father and mother, brother and sister, friend closer than a brother, sweet presence of wife or child—all these, in will at least, perhaps in act, he will have to surrender. They may fall off from him, in feeling, or by death. He may have to sever the tie, because Christ bids him go, or because they will not follow him for Christ. But he shall have compensation. There is a family—no man can number it—in earth and heaven, of which he becomes a member when he becomes a Christian. God is its Father, Christ is its Head; holy Angels are its elder brothers; saints, martyrs, and Apostles, all good men, dead and living, are its inmates and its kinsfolk; earth is its compass, heaven is its home; and whosoever believes in Christ, whosoever has the Holy Spirit in him, enters at once upon the affections and the sympathies of all these: every Christian whom he meets and whom he works with is his brother or his sister: every Christian matron who cheers him by her womanly kindness is his mother, and every Christian boy whom he influences by his manly love is straightway his child : extend, expand this kinsmanship through all space and all time, and you will see why Jesus Christ should say that the man who gives up, or is willing to give up, the natural, wins a hundredfold in the spiritual —is a richer man, even in relationships, than he was, or could be, without Christ—may well say, as he sets off earth against heaven, I am the gainer beyond words—those things which were my prizes and my treasures, *I count them all but dross and loss for Christ.*

Delightful must it have been, to the great heart of Saint Paul, when his name was cast out as evil by family and country, to find wheresoever he carried the Name, a new brotherhood and sisterhood created for him. *Phœbe our sister...Andronicus and Junias my kinsmen...Gaius mine host, and Quartus my brother...Rufus chosen in the Lord, and her who is his mother and mine*—thus he runs through, in a letter to one Church, not yet visited, the list of his new, his Christian, relations: we feel, as we read, the force of the *hundredfold now in this time;* we begin to understand the text as something having indeed *the promise of this life;* we pause perhaps, and scarcely (I think) with tearless eye, at that one anonymous title, *his mother and mine:* one faithful woman in the Roman congregation—her name, surely, is in the Book of Life—had the honour above all honour to be a *mother* to that toiling, yearning, most loving, most loveable man.

This is that *love of the brethren* of which

St John writes that without it life itself is death. We talk much of charity; we sing its praises as the synonym of good nature, of toleration, of vagueness, too often of indifference: assuredly we do not pass to it, as alone we can safely pass, through this other —through the love of the brethren. *Add*, St Peter says, *to brotherly kindness charity. Supply* the one, he says in his own Greek, *through* the other. Let the love of Christian for Christian expand and spread itself till it embraces Greek and Barbarian, till it loves for the sake of Christ even those unloving ones for whom nevertheless Christ died.

But before even this true charity stands the family love of the Church. Let us make more of this. There are lonely people on this great earth—how could this be if they knew of the text, if they read, if they pleaded it? Health, position, circumstance, accident, may debar them from its full fruition. They live perhaps alone, and 'must live, so far as the speech and the sight go, not only of the natural but of the spiritual brotherhood. Still, when they think of it; when they know that only the speech or the sight is wanting; when they remember the great universe, the visible and the invisible, instinct and teeming with this sympathy, which is, being interpreted, God's love reflected and echoed everywhere in the love of God; can they not take courage? Lost brother and sister, lost father and mother, replaced a hundredfold now in this time—only just out of sight—hereafter to be manifested, in all the beauty and in all the plenitude of the everlasting home—shall it not comfort? Every act of worship a meeting of this family; every prayer, every aspiration, an exercise of this sympathy, a prognostication of this union—well might St John write, *We know that we have passed into life, because we love the brethren*, and then conversely, lest any should torture himself as to his possession of this evidential love, *By this we know that we love the children of God, when we love God.* Either of the two loves—so intertwined, so inseparable, are they—shall attest, shall prove, them both.

The festival on which we are assembled is the festival of brotherly love. Two Apostles, brothers perhaps first by birth, brothers (it may have been) of the Lord Himself by birth, have separately left all for His sake and the Gospel's; and they have found themselves again brothers, to Him and to each other, not after the flesh but after the Spirit. The Church has wedded the names in one commemoration, as the perpetual symbol of the consecrated *two and two. He sent his disciples,* He sends them still, *two and two before His face into every city and place whither He Himself would come.* It is thus that Cambridge has constituted her Delhi Mission. I quote the words: 'Many advantages may be expected from sending out an organized band of men prepared to live and labour together in one foreign field—concentration of effort and subdivision of labour, continuity of teaching, economy of means, leisure for literary work (in reaching through the Press the educated classes of India), and frequent opportunities of united devotion.'

> These are the tones to brace and cheer
>   The lonely watcher of the fold,
> When nights are dark, and foemen near,
>   When visions fade and hearts grow cold.

Brethren! let us resolve—you, more especially, whose life is still young—you, who can do so much to give the tone to the religion, to the theology, of a generation which shall take our place on God's earth—never to narrow this love. Let us never refuse a share of it to any one who will have it. Let us rejoice in the thought that the kingdom is wider than our knowledge, grander and more generous than our stipulations. *Firstfruits of His creatures*, this is our designation. Let us hope, and let us pray, that, *if the firstfruits are holy, so shall be the lump.* Lord, hasten it in Thy time!

In this vast field of thought much must be left unnoticed. Of two things passed over I am conscious.

With persecutions. Note that characteristic candour of the Gospel, first exemplified by its Lord, which will entrap no man into His service; which will set full in view before each one of us the sorrows and the sacrifices, and then say, Count well the cost; and, if you do put your hand to the plough, look not back.

Also that overwhelming word in which all is summed up, *And in the world to come eternal life.* This one thing is less for speech than for silence. *No man hath ascended up into heaven,* that he should come back to say to his brethren, *I saw the holy city,* and lo, it is this, and this.

We must turn to things less high above out of our sight, and remind you of a practical duty, which I have to-day, as in many past years, to press earnestly upon your attention.

The University dwells in a Town, and the Church of the Town is a suppliant to-day to the Church of the University. Christians with Christians plead not ever in vain; and assuredly the Town, if in some sense injuriously affected in past time by the near neighbourhood of much carelessness and some licentiousness, is now deeply the debtor of the University, not more for substantial prosperity, than for noble, magnificent Christian example.

Of all the signs of spiritual vitality in our beloved University, I count none so conclusive, as its efforts, of the last half century and conspicuously of the last ten years, in behalf of the spiritual life of the Town. A few days ago you were celebrating the jubilee of the University Sunday School for the poor children of Cambridge. A touching festival of song and thanksgiving commemorated on that occasion the Advent and the Sacrifice of *God with us;* and no heart that could feel was insensible that day to the realization of the Emmanuel Presence in the work of those young men— young when they wrought in it, now of hoar hairs many of them, and many fallen on sleep— who gave of their precious hours, of their intervals of anxious intellectual labour, in the fifty years that are passed, to the enterprise of evangelizing Cambridge through its little ones and through its homes.

In comparison with such proofs of a personal devotion, where shall we place the mere struggling to listen to a popular voice, the mere crowding of Churches where either ritual, song, or preaching, exercises a powerful attraction upon sympathetic assemblies?

To-day you are reminded of a movement of our own generation to maintain additional Ministers for the poor parishes of Barnwell and Chesterton; in other words, to carry the preaching of the Gospel into the streets and lanes of these suburbs, by the instrumentality of faithful men acting in entire conformity with the rules of Apostolical order. It is an evidence, second not even to that which has been named, of the awakening zeal and love of the University towards its less privileged neighbours. I would bid you to study the records of the movement, to thank God for it, and then to help it, as you can, with your sympathy, your alms, your prayers.

I am bound to tell you that very much of its efficiency for the year that is now running its course will depend upon the offerings of your bounty to-day. Nothing would be easier than for this Congregation to place it by a single effort beyond risk and beyond anxiety.

More than once I have ventured to ask you—and once at least you kindly listened to me—to take care that the collection at these doors should not fall short of a hundred pounds. Less than this will leave us still in suspense, still pondering the sad question which of our grants to those four destitute Parishes must be withdrawn, diminished, or left in arrear. And think with yourselves, dear brethren, how small a sacrifice it would cost you, of anything that you really value as intelligent Christian men, to make such an offering this afternoon as would represent but two shillings apiece from the great Congregation which I look upon from this Pulpit.

It is very interesting, and to Christian hearts very encouraging, to notice how the supply of one spiritual want leads on to the demand for another; how, when you have given a Pastor, the people cry out for a Church, and by that second cry tell you that their souls thank and bless you for having heard or for having anticipated the first.

We have been reading, this week, the account of the re-opening of a great Cathedral, in which, at an interval of five centuries, a new nave has been added to the old choir, and the fabric stands out at last in all the completeness and grandeur of its original design. On a small scale, indeed, but with a more urgent necessity, we would ask you for a like work of perfecting in a Church of this Town. The Church of St Barnabas is still a fragment—a naveless chancel: the people throng that little area; they want space for worshippers that would be—will you help to give it them? Will you come forward, those *in whom such a heart is*, and collect for this work, in your Colleges, and among your friends?

O the blessedness of work done for Jesus Christ! Done in sincerity, done in simplicity, done in love, it shall not lack its reward. *A hundredfold now in this time—in the world to come,* who shall speak it?

When Jesus Christ uttered the glorious promise on which we have dwelt, He thought it necessary to couple it with one caution. I would humbly follow that Divine example, and say one closing word upon the verse following the text—

But many that are first shall be last, and the last first.

It is a caution, and it is an encouragement. Both were needed then: Peter himself needed both—the one on the instant, when he was boasting; the other, a few weeks after, when he was bitterly weeping: can either this or that be needless here to-day?

Many shall be—first last. Where is boasting?

How sudden, how insidious, is the entrance of the foe! The very consciousness of standing is of the nature of a fall. The very thought,

God, I thank thee, may be the Pharisee worship—that prayerless thanksgiving which goes not home justified.

There are those who once ran well: who, what, hath hindered them? What special weakness, indolence, temptation? God knoweth—yes, they know! To-day they are laggards, sluggards, rebels, renegades. Shall they rise again? Shall that stupid sleep, that deadly lust, that fatal infidelity, ever be shaken off, cast out, recovered from? Shall they one day be pleading—O let it be this night—pleading in their own behalf the promise, *Many shall be— last first?*

Whose memory can adduce no instance of this? That young boy, once so light-hearted and joyous—you saw him play, you heard him jest, in the days of his ignorance: *you* were then the serious one; you augured ill, perhaps, for his hereafter: in early youth you lost sight of him—where is he now? A Christian soldier, a Christian Missionary, a Christian Martyr; rejoicing in Christ here, or sleeping in Christ for long years in some rough Crimean or Indian or African grave.

But we all want the prophecy—want it for the safe standing, want it for the possible rising—*Many that are last shall be first.*

What morning breaks upon me not among the hindmost? When is the morning prayer light-hearted, when is the evening prayer jubilant, for any one of us? O, if the hope were only for the hopeful, if the race were only to the swift, if the battle only to the strong, who, who could persevere? It is the thought of Him who stooped from His heaven of holiness and of glory, to fetch the distant nigh and to say *Last first*—it is this which keeps me so much as struggling. *Lord, I believe; help Thou mine unbelief*—this is my best. He casts not out this: He seems to bid even this look upward.

Then let us love Him for His great love. He came not to call the righteous: then perhaps He came to call even me.

VII.

THREE TYPES OF CHARACTER—ENTHUSIASM, RELUCTANCE, COMPROMISE.

VII.

THREE TYPES OF CHARACTER— ENTHUSIASM, RELUCTANCE, COMPROMISE.

LUKE ix. 62.

No man, having put his hand to the plough, and looking back, is fit for the kingdom of God.

THIS verse, like the third of the three narratives which it closes, is found only in St Luke. It gives great completeness to the exhibition of human character in its dealing with Christ and the Gospel, which is the subject of the paragraph. *That the thoughts of many hearts may be revealed* is stated by the old man, holding in his arms the Infant

Saviour, as the purpose, no less than the result, of that 'gainsaying' which, he prophesied, should everywhere attend Him. We have here the thoughts of three hearts revealed: and seeing that human nature is the same in all times, and that the treatment of Jesus Christ is in reality the test of all lives, and that there are here before me a number of young lives yet to be shaped and moulded as to their course and as to their destination, I trust that a few plain words may not be unseasonable this afternoon upon the three characters delineated in this passage of the Book of God for perpetual conviction, correction, and education in righteousness.

1. In the first instance we have an example of that enthusiasm which Jesus Christ awakened, by His teaching, character, and presence, in hearts capable of appreciating the true, the great, the beautiful, the Divine. If St Luke gives the right place to this incident,

we might imagine that it was our Lord's language about the Samaritan village—His rebuke to the two brothers who would call fire from heaven to avenge its inhospitable conduct—His saying, *Ye know not what manner of spirit ye are of; for the Son of Man is not come to destroy men's lives, but to save them*—which elicited this eager and chivalrous proposal, *Lord, I will follow Thee whithersoever Thou goest.*

But it needed not one particular manifestation of the glory and beauty of Jesus Christ to account for that outburst of devotion. It must have been the feeling of a thousand hearts, as men tracked His footsteps along the lanes and hill-sides of Galilee, and listened day by day to the gracious words which proceeded out of His mouth. We know what it is, in poor human experience, to feel the whole soul stirred within us by the sight of a life wholly given to the service of God in charity, or by the hearing of words of loving entreaty from lips evidently giving forth that which was a life before it was a doctrine. We know how one man devoting himself to the cause of Christ, in India, in Africa, in New Zealand, has had power to draw after him by the magnet of sympathy tens and hundreds of other men, whose souls were of that higher order, in point of love and in point of purity, which can respond to a call not of this world, and find it none the less persuasive if it demands of them the sacrifice of their all. Judge ye, from this experience, what must have been, to hearts capable of it, the influence of Jesus Christ, present in person to point the way, and able without presumption to propose Himself to His hearers as at once the Guide and the Companion, the Light of the living and the Life of the dead.

There are those—can we doubt it?—amongst the occupants of these galleries, who have many times in these last ten or fifteen years felt just the impulse of this young scribe. There have been days of cloudless beauty, in the world of nature and in the world of feeling, when they have longed for a satisfying love and an open heaven. There have been days of strong conviction, of powerful impression, of resolute effort, when they have aspired to a noble life, and none the less if it should have in it the abandonment of luxury and the treading underfoot of fame. There have been days of deep sorrow, of felt loneliness, it may be of secret self-shame, when they could have given their all, on the instant, for one word with the holy and merciful Saviour, who is said to have said on earth, *Come unto me all ye that are weary and heavy laden*—and *If any man thirst, let him come unto me, and drink.*

And they know and feel this day, in their heart and in their soul, that such moments were not their worst but their best; not moments to be ashamed of, but moments in which God was moving in them to quicken the very life which would make them God-like. O compare with such moments the intervening months and years of stupid droning, silly trifling, or cowardly sinning. Pray that such moments may come again to you. Pray that the cry may rise again to your lips, as you plan the long life, as you forecast the infinite future, *Lord, I will follow Thee whithersoever Thou goest.*

And yet, in this context, that prayer is not welcomed. We are reminded again and again, in reading the Gospels, first of the fragmentary, and secondly of the parabolical, character of the Evangelic history. Men come and go, appear and disappear, speak and are silent, without one word to tell us the whence and the whither, the significance of the speech or the significance of the silence. It is so in all Scripture. We are not intended to settle the question of questions for dead men any more than for the living. Each actor on the stage of the Bible has his part, and he plays it. He speaks for admonition, in some way and in some sense; but he tarries not to be interrogated concerning his history as a whole, or concerning his destiny in the judgment.

It is so with this Scribe. Whether he spoke unadvisedly, and was rebuffed by Christ's answer—or whether he laid to heart the warning, and yet stood to his offer—or whether he departed for the time, but went to return—this we know not. There is parable in miracle—there is parable too in history: as parable we best read it, because then its lessons are for all time, and the lifeless page becomes a voice vocal to the living.

Thou sayest—and they are good words—*Lord, I will follow Thee.* But hast thou thought of this—the unrest of the Christian 'following?' *Foxes have holes, birds of the air have* nests; only the Son of Man hath not where to lay His head.

We must not add or diminish where Jesus Christ has spoken. This is His own description of the homelessness of His life of Ministry. Once He had a home. We picture Him to ourselves, during all those long years of preparation for His work, the central object in a home of humble industry but of sleepless love. This home He had left, for charity and for ministry, for man and God. Now He had no home. Such attention as was shown, by Pharisee from one motive, by the sisters of Bethany from another motive, He accepted when it offered itself: but many days there was none such, and that absence also of service He accepted in its season. He who would follow Him must share with Him the service, and the lack of service—hast thou counted the cost?

Brethren, we read the parable of the homelessness of Jesus Christ, as preparing us, His disciples now, for a life, I will not say of restlessness, but I will say, of unrest. It is the trial of trials to His people. Want of home is nothing to it. O, it is the feeling of being wanderers, not in the letter but in the spirit, which makes the Christian life hard. For some, indeed, it fulfils itself quite literally. There are those, still—blessed be God for it—who will go forth, *taking nothing*—purse, scrip, and staff forgotten—that they may just follow the footsteps of Jesus Christ. There is a Bishop now in Australia—I saw him consecrated more than thirty years ago in Westminster Abbey—he has never seen England since that year: childless, wifeless, homeless, he has just been the Missionary Bishop, living for Christ and His people: now he is struck down by paralysis—he will die there. These are the men who in act as well as in will, in the letter as well as in the spirit, follow Christ whithersoever He goeth. *The Son of Man hath not where to lay His head*—wilt thou follow Him *everywhere?* Think of it twice ere thou speakest the *whithersoever.* Think of it twice—yes, but think of it. It is a blessed life—blessed, and rich in blessing.

We shall not escape the unrest by escaping the homelessness. All who speak the word, *Lord, I will follow,* must lay their account for this trial. You may think you have found your rest : perhaps in some English Parsonage, beautiful and homelike ; within reach of dear friends, and surrounded by an attached people. Perhaps in a well-digested system of traditional theology; text balanced by text, authorities well weighed, and a long line of worthies attesting the correctness of the Shibboleth and the completeness of the doctrine. Perhaps in the full assurance, either of a baptismal regeneration, needing only to be lived up to ; or else of a conscious conversion, to which you can assign both place and hour, both source and course.

Thus you may be saying, The outward homelessness may come to me, if God will; but the inward rest is sure: *I shall never be moved; Thou, Lord, of Thy goodness hast made my hill so strong.*

Enjoy, while you may, Christian Scribe, the rest and the home, outward or inward. Yet mark Christ's words, *The Son of Man hath not where to lay His head.* Read His words spiritually, and be prepared—I say but this—be prepared to find thy moorings shifted and thy cables severed; to find, if thou wilt open thine ears, many voices in them, compelling thee to enquire; to find, if thou wilt open thine heart, many voices in it, saying, *This is not thy rest—* not here, not here, is absolute quietness—not here, not here, is the perfect peace. The trial of the Christian is the homelessness of Jesus. *Always bearing about in the body* the unrest of the Master, that the rest also of the Master may be manifested in the storm-tossed soul.

Enthusiasm is one of the 'thoughts of hearts' revealed by contact with Jesus. He meets it with warning. None shall come after Him by mistake or in misunderstanding. *The Son of Man hath not where to lay His head*, and they that would follow Him must expect to fare likewise. The true 'enthusiast,' which is to say, the man who has the fire of God in him, will come, for all that: nay, the very repulsion has attraction in it; *the servant is not greater than his Lord*, and he would not rest while his Lord wanders.

2. The next case is the direct opposite. St Luke alone gives it its full significance by assigning the initiative here to Christ. *He said unto another, Follow me.* And the man makes excuse.

Even upon earth there was sovereignty in the voice of Jesus Christ. *When thou comest in Thy kingdom*, were words addressed to Him on the Cross. *Thou sayest that I am a king,* was His own answer to His judge.

Thus was it in that call by which He gathered to Him His twelve Apostles. He passed, one day, by the counting-house of a rich official; spoke the word, *Follow me,* to a man as little expecting it, as little prepared for it, as any one of you, rising from his bed this morning, was prepared for a summons to America or to China; and there was that in the tone which carried authority as well as persuasion, and the person addressed instantly abandoned His gainful calling, and, after one solemn feast of farewell and welcome, became one of the disciples, one of the Apostles, at last one of the Evangelists, of the Man who had not where to lay His head. Sovereignty was in the summons, and the heart heard it.

Some such preferment was offered in the case before us. The gracious, the awful, *Follow me,* was spoken, and the man accosted by it was bidden to enter that innermost circle which was first to take the impress, and then to represent the likeness, of a God manifested in the flesh.

The call which was not for the enthusiast was for him. Wonderful discrimination! This man wants, what the other required not, a startling demand for an instantaneous decision. This man was halting between two opinions. Sovereignty itself speaks here to an ambiguous subject. The grandest of careers is opened before this life. But there is an impediment.

We take the reply literally, and conceive of this person as having left in his home the lifeless body of a father, to which it is a primary duty to pay the rites of burial. It may have been to soothe the sorrow of that recent parting that he had mingled with the crowd surrounding the Saviour. The voice of Jesus has ever had music in it for the mourner: the brief pause between the death and the funeral could not better be filled than by a visit to the Man of Sorrows, who made Himself felt also, before He verbally claimed the title, as *the Resurrection and the Life.*

How natural then—we must say it—that the *Follow me* should elicit the answer, itself submissive and reverent, *Lord, suffer me first to go and bury my father.* Nature prompts, duty requires, religion orders, that, in death as in life, a son should honour his father: how can Christ, Himself the best of sons, Himself even from the Cross caring for His mother, hesitate to say, *Go and do it,* even if He should add in the same breath, *Then return and follow?* Which of us has not felt the severity of that hard saying, *Let the dead bury their dead, but go thou and preach the kingdom of God?* Has the tenderness of Jesus Christ for once left Him? Has He who wept at the grave which He was instantly to open no word of sympathy for this orphan son, nothing but the harsh order to dash away his tears and go and preach? Even the ordained man, pledged once, twice, and thrice, to the Church's Ministry, counts it no lack of service if he gives a Sunday of silence to the memory of a lost wife or child, feels that this silence may preach more eloquently to the living than a hundred Sermons, is itself a tribute of reverence to the Master who both gives and takes away. Yet that Master speaks here in other tones, *Let the dead bury their dead—go thou, and preach.*

We presume not to say what special reasons there may have been in this instance for a peremptoriness which could brook no delay. But of this we are sure that Jesus Christ is here teaching us in parable, and that we can all, if we will, hear Him.

There is one thing, He says, yet more important than any competing or conflicting duty. That one thing is the reign of God in man's heart, and the establishment of that reign first of all in thine own. Be jealous of anything which comes to thee saying, 'Christ may call, but listen first to me.' This thing may take the shape of duty. It may parade before thee wishes, conveniences, comforts of friends, when the voice is strong in thee for missionary service. It may expostulate with thee as concerning old age, infirm health, tender affection, in one who gave thee being and has a right in thee to every place but one. It may say, Wait but the ten years, or the five years, which alone can separate thee from the death and from the burial, and then follow whithersoever He goeth.

And we know, brethren, how deep is the love of Christ for earth's affections, which He created, which He consecrated, which He felt. O, it is not because a particular ministry or a particular mission is painful to those near and dear to us, that therefore it is Christ's call. He would not have one real duty neglected, or one willing wound inflicted, or one wanton void created, on the plea that He has spoken and must be obeyed. Men deceive themselves sometimes in this direction, and misname wilfulness sacrifice and cruelty Christianity.

But this is not so common as another delinquency; which is, the ingenuity of discovering obstacles, the fertility of multiplying impediments, in the way of visible openings, clear calls, and conscious capacities. It is not necessary that a whole family of sons should all remain in sight of ever so dear a home. It is not reasonable that they who reconcile themselves to the gift of one child to military service or commercial enterprise, knowing that it may involve long, perhaps life-long, separations—perils, perhaps of premature death, in the accidents, by sea and land, of distant duty—should only count it impossible to spare another to Christ Himself; should only plead, *Suffer him first to bury his father*, when the devotion asked is *for Christ's sake and the Gospel's*, and the work to be done is the seeking in far-off islands of Christ's *sheep that are scattered abroad*.

Then it is that the stern mandate, *Let the dead bury their dead*, awakens into a righteous imperiousness—even if we hear it say, There is one thing more urgent than a funeral, there is one relationship closer still than the filial, there is one tie of duty more binding yet than any natural. Let the dead bury themselves rather than cause oblivion of that: at least leave the dead in soul to bury the dead in body—at least leave for ever to a world dead in sin that office which is so dear to it, of the mutual burying, heart helping heart to forget the eternal, life encouraging life to deify the temporal.

Yes, Christ's sayings, as the Psalmist says of God's judgments, *are a great deep*. They have in them a thousand meanings, ten thousand applications: and then first do we at all sound the depths of this saying, when we read death itself spiritually, and understand it to warn us against *that* kind of burying which is the heaping high and higher upon each other the mould of corrupt affection and inordinate passion, of the worship of wealth and the idolatry of intellect, of the perpetual postponement of seriousness, and the most deceptive yet most persuasive insinuation, *We have made a covenant with death, and with hell are we at agreement.*

This is the very occupation of earth and earth's children. Against this is the trumpet of the Gospel vainly sounded, in ears which accept the word that they may take out of it the meaning. Against this *burying of their dead by the dead* no protest is one half so efficacious as that of a new life entering into some separately convinced soul; a new self-dedication to Christ's absolute service, at home or abroad, of one who has heard with the inward ear His *Follow me,* and has been made *willing in the day of His power* to obey.

Then it shall matter little, comparatively, to the great cause, whether this land or that land shall employ the service; whether it be given to the first evangelization or the second— to the annunciation of Christ where He is not yet named, or to the task, of no inferior magnitude, of making Christ real where for generations He has been nominal. *Follow me* is a voice of infinite compass: it will define itself in its season—it may be more than once over—to the singly listening soul.

3. Enthusiasm cautioned, reluctance stimulated—what third 'heart's thought' remains for Christ's discipline?

It is a character wonderfully composite which St Luke here presents to us. It partakes of both the former. Like the first, it volunteers to follow: like the second, it petitions for delay. *And another also said, Lord, I will follow Thee; but let me first go bid them farewell, which are at home at my house.*

We have named the first character Enthusiasm, and we have named the second character Reluctance: we must call the third character Compromise.

This man offers to follow Jesus. Something, though in fainter and slighter degree, of the attraction which drew the young Scribe has been felt also here. The holy doctrine of the Saviour has awakened an echo in the conscience: the moral beauty of the Saviour has found its appreciation in the heart.

Lord, I will follow Thee. Despised and rejected, wanderer and exile, I will follow Thee. Thou hast words of eternal life; my soul is athirst for them: yes, I will follow Thee. *What lacks he yet?*

We say nothing of the omission of the *whithersoever Thou goest:* we take that as implied. It is not omission that we notice, but addition. There is a clause here which was not in the first. The volunteer stipulates, the enthusiast procrastinates. He will follow—*but he must do one thing first.*

Like the two brothers in the paragraph above, he might have invoked the precedent of Elijah, who, instead of rebuking, encouraged Elisha in this sort of preliminary farewell; even when he had cast upon him the prophetic mantle, said, *What have I done to thee?* and granted instantly the request of natural duty, *Let me, I pray thee, kiss my father and my mother, and then I will follow thee.* Just such was the prayer, *Lord, I will follow Thee—but let me first go bid them farewell, which are at home at my house.*

But the prayer is not granted. Doubtless the Searcher of hearts saw something in this heart which made the adieu perilous. At all events, He was teaching for all time; and the parable for all time is this, *No man, having put his hand to the plough, and looking back, is fit for the kingdom of God.*

There may be an impulse of good, which is short of a resolution: there may be a resolution of good, which is short of a principle: there may even be a principle of good, which breaks down in practice. *The spirit may be willing, and yet the flesh weak.* We cannot trust ourselves with these farewells, at least till one question has been answered, *Who* are 'they at home?'

Even natural affection, the purest and the most human, has had power to divert from Christ's service, in some difficult, some enterprising form, the heart that had just sworn the 'sacrament.' There are those who have put their hand to the plough, and then looked back. There are young men, pledged from childhood to the Ministry, who have broken that pledge at the University. There are young Clergymen, self-destined, self-devoted, to the highest Ministry, the work of the foreign Evangelist, who have found the spell of home, the spell of love, too strong for them, and in the very going to bid farewell have been seduced into a permanent looking back. There are men, young and old, who have consecrated themselves to the Church of the world—have 'set to their seal,' as well as 'put their hand,' to the engagement of a life's sacrifice—and have found it impossible, with their measure of grace, to hold the purpose and to be faithful to it till death. The sands of earth, the fields of the Church, are covered with the print of these backward footsteps: they have taken the romance out of Missions; they have lowered the standard of the very word devotion.

Yet these men may have done nothing wrong. They may have been good men; not only *saved as by fire* with *the work burned*, but leaving something done towards the everlasting Temple.

Compromise is scarcely the name for *these* withdrawals. We go back to our question,

Who are they at the house, to whom the farewell must be spoken ere the man can follow Jesus Christ?

I know well enough that it is not only natural affection which bars the way of devotion. There is a procrastination strangely blending with enthusiasm, and it has all manner of motives and all manner of excuses.

It may be too much to suppose—it is too much, certainly, to take for granted—that all we are, in any true sense, so much as pledged and plighted to follow. The word has not yet been spoken between us and Christ, *Lord, I will follow Thee.* A thousand doubts have sprung up, and they have not been grappled with, who and what Christ is—*whether* indeed He is, except it be as a temporary dweller in the past—a saintly name, a perfect life, a bright, for us a too bright, example. Therefore we can have no dealing with Him: we cannot treat with Him on the footing of the 'I' and

'Thou:' we cannot speak to the non-existent; we cannot follow, save in most distant, most shadowy imitation, One whose footsteps, now at least, go nowhither.

And yet there is that in us all which would give worlds for just such a One. If He is not, there is a blank, there is a void, there is a darkness which may be felt. Thus much of evidence He has: without this witness He has not left Himself. We count it a proof above proof, that, made as we are made, there is an idea in us, there is an instinct in us, there is a want in us, of Jesus Christ. *Lord, to whom shall we go if Thou be not?* is an outcry of the creature, eloquent of the Creator: that pure, that sublime appetite, for the Godman—in other words, for an Incarnation of the Divine—is an argument, for such as believe in love, that the Father has revealed Himself in the Son.

Thousands believe this—could therefore

deal with Jesus Christ as the Risen, the Living One—and yet interpose something before the doing so. It is to these the text speaks.

There is something in your home which cannot stay there with Jesus; something to which you must say farewell ere you follow Him. What is it?

There is something each day (who has not found it so?) between us and duty; most of all, between us and spiritual duty—the duty of refreshing and strengthening the spirit by communion with the Father, of seeking Him whom to know is eternal life. Mere indolence of heart, mere laziness of body—a book, a letter, a newspaper, a moment's converse with a friend—something there is which prompts the saying, 'I will follow Thee, but—just this first:' and of this too, this small, this insignificant postponement, Christ says, It is unfit, it is unsuitable, for a disciple of the kingdom.

But at certain periods of life (who has not found it so?) there is something more than this between us and duty. *Fearfully and wonderfully made,* is the Psalmist's estimate of the mechanism of this body: yet more true is it of the life. When is anything quite done with, that has once been? One incident of the life's past—one weakness, one folly, one sin—how importunate, how imperishable, how immortal, is it! Ghosts of old habit, when shall I have laid you? Demons of old sinning, when shall I have exorcised you? These are the things—I had almost said, these are the persons—'at home at my house,' to which I would fain say farewell ere I finally devote myself. And in that *saying farewell* there is oftentimes a *looking backward.* Compromise may lurk in the stipulation, and he that would follow Jesus can only make sure of it by following on the instant.

Finally, there is a moment in each life,

when it is called to a decision of what kind and of what spirit it will be. It is this which gives its peculiar solemnity to a scene and to an occasion like the present. For it is here, it is now, that lives are determining themselves, for this world and for that which is to come. We ourselves can recall Sermons preached forty years since from the Pulpit of a great University, of which the echo is in us to this day and to this hour. It is not given to all men to speak words of everlasting impression: but the cause of the impression is the reality of the crisis; and the crisis is ever new, so long as the young life shall be repeating itself year by year in the old places—so long as God shall be sending forth His Spirit to renew, and bidding each man of each generation go forth to his work and to his labour till the evening. May it please Him, by any instrumentality, to put forth His Omnipotent grace in the determination of multitudes of these lives for a service the noblest of all and the most delightful. May a new enthusiasm, all of grace, kill in us the lethargy of the self-pleasing, and the reluctance of the half-heart. May we count the cost, and yet follow—may we put our hand to the plough, and never look back. Let the dead past bury its dead, and let the living responsible present sow for the everlasting future an immortality of joy and glory.

VIII.

THE PROPER ATTITUDE FOR RELIGIOUS ENQUIRY.

VIII.

THE PROPER ATTITUDE FOR RELIGIOUS ENQUIRY.

Psalm cxxxi. 2, 3.

I do not exercise myself in great matters, which are too high for me.

But I refrain my soul, and keep it low.

The words are beautiful and suggestive. They speak for themselves, as to their suitableness to this great Festival[1], the crowning day of the Church's year—and not less to the life of souls, training here for the service of a generation, and for the capability of an immortal being.

It will not be necessary to enter to-day into

[1] Trinity Sunday.

the vexed question of the title, *A song of Degrees*, prefixed to each one of the fifteen Psalms which follow immediately upon the hundred and nineteenth. Whether it is a musical term, or a poetical term, or a local term; whether it points to some peculiarity in the chant to which the Psalm was to be set—or to some peculiarity in the composition, rising from point to point upon some predominant word, the keynote of the thought—or to some particular spot, whether stair or gallery, in the temple courts where it was to be sung; is a matter of no moment to us to-day, when, if the choice be free to us, we would rather look upon this as in a different sense a Song of Ascents; one of the 'Hymns of the going up'—whether of the delivered exile, returning to Jerusalem from Babylon—or of the Galilæan pilgrim, seeking the holy city for one of the periodical feasts, and cheering the morning start or the noontide pause or the evening resting with one of those

Songs of Zion which shall answer for him the appropriate question, *Wherewith shall I come before the Lord and bow myself before the High God? Who shall ascend into the hill of the Lord, or who shall rise up in His holy place?*

And then the Psalm will become one of the 'shadows cast before' of the Divine teaching of Jesus. *Two men went up into the temple to pray,* and the one that *went down to his house justified* was the man of a humble spirit; the man who *stood afar off,* with downcast eyes, and *smote upon his breast, saying, God be merciful to me a sinner. My heart is not haughty, nor mine eyes lofty: I have not walked in great things, things too wonderful for me: but I refrain my soul, and keep it low.*

The expressions are striking and exquisite. *I have calmed and hushed my soul. I have calmed*—properly, *I have levelled*—my soul: I have made it smooth and even; like the field that has been furrowed by the plough and is now laid level by the harrow; or like the sea that has been tossed by storm and tempest and is now soothed and stilled again into calm. And then, once more, *I have hushed my soul —made it silent,* is the exact thought, from its clamouring and its murmuring—*like the weaned child upon the breast of his mother;* taught his first lesson of denial and disappointment, and now beginning to acquiesce in the discipline, if he may but 'cling still, in fond helplessness, to the bosom of his one friend.' Even thus—such is the strong figure of the original—even thus my soul—the living moving heart of feeling and affection, represented for the moment as distinct (like intellect, or memory, or conscience) from the 'I myself I' of the man—my soul rests, as it were, upon my bosom from all its wanderings and all its soarings, and learns at last to submit itself to that quieter, safer, holier employment, which is the love of that which God has commanded, and the desire of that which God has promised. *I have calmed and hushed my soul: As the weaned child lies my soul upon me. Wait, O Israel, for the Lord, from henceforth even for ever.*

I do not exercise myself in great matters, which are too high for me.

The text carries us into the region of thought. It recognizes the responsibility of thinking. It presupposes the possibility of choosing and refusing in the entertainment of subjects. It implies that there are wholesome topics of thought and unwholesome; and that a man is just as much bound to discriminate in the things he thinks of, as in the employment of his hours, the formation of his habits, or the selection of his friends.

In this general statement all probably will agree. Doubtless there are here and there persons of exceptionally feeble will, who avow that they have no control over their thoughts; that they cannot avoid those rovings and saunterings of the mind, which lead to all manner of loose and corrupt imaginations, not to be justified yet not to be prevented. The stern moralist and the gentle Christian agree in regarding such helplessness as either a crime or a madness; the result either of frightful neglect, or else of a moral malformation as mysterious as it is miserable. At all events, no safe place can be found in human society for one who professes himself impotent over the mind which makes the life.

Most men know perfectly well that they can control thought; that they can 'make the porter watch' the comings in as well as the goings out, the entrances of thought as well as the exits of action.

But the remarkable thing in the text is the enlargement of the responsibility of the self-control, from the nature and quality, to what we may call the scale and size, of the thoughts.

We can well believe that the holy and

devout Psalmist did not suffer his heart to entertain licentious and lascivious thoughts; that he did not compose these sweet songs, or wend his way towards Zion, with the love of sin allowed in him, or with the power of sin reigning.

He speaks not of low but of high thoughts, not of grovelling but of soaring imaginations, as the disallowed and discountenanced inmates.

And there can be no doubt that there is a danger in this direction. There are not only evil desires, sinful lustings, to make frightful havoc of the life and of the soul: there are also speculations and rovings of thought, which give no other warning of their nature than this, that they belong to districts and regions beyond and above us; that they are fatal to the quietness and the silence of the spirit; that they cannot be entertained without reawakening those restless and unsatisfied yearnings which were just beginning to still themselves on the bosom of Infinite Love.

Of this sort, sometimes, are the ambitions of this life. Ambition has a use as well as an abuse. St Paul himself, who had counted all things loss, yet, thrice in his Epistles, speaks of ambition as his life. We use ambition in our education. We count anything better than that stagnation of the being, which begins in idleness and ends in sensuality. We waken up the drowsy energies by proposing to them prizes of effort. We bid them even 'strive for masteries.' Competition itself, though it be the near kinsman of that *emulation* which St Paul puts among *works of the flesh*, is yet enlisted among the soldiers of Jesus Christ, if so be it may sublime itself at last into an effort which desires no man's crown.

Nevertheless we all feel that there is an ambition 'which o'erleaps itself,' not more in the arrogance of its successes than in the extravagance of its expectations. There are men who would have been, not only happier, but greater, if they had been less ambitious. There are men whose humbler efforts would at least have been respected, but whose more adventurous soarings have ended only in ridicule.

Especially is this true in the province of the intellect. We have known little men living with great men till nothing could content them but being great themselves. They have breathed an intellectual atmosphere till they have imagined an inspiration. There was no man to say to them, or they heeded not the warning, 'Learn of the wise—but be not many masters.' They began by reproducing—they ended in imitating. The very words of the wise came not 'mended' but damaged 'from that tongue.' They stood on tiptoe, but they were dwarfs still. The same men, contented with reality—which, in their case, was mediocrity—might have done a useful, if not an illustrious work in the generation which they were set, not to illuminate, but to serve. As men of industry, men of information, men of sense, they might have been eyes to the blind and feet to the lame. They might have been teachers in schools of which they could not be founders—handers on of that torch of truth which it was not given them to kindle. After all, the debt of the passing generation must be more to toil than to genius: this was their measure, this ought to have been their goal. They ought to have said—and they would have been gainers by saying it—*I will not exercise myself in great matters: they are too high for me. I will calm and hush my soul.*

That which is true in the ambitions of this life, whether professional or intellectual, is not less true in religion. It might seem that the Psalmist wrote of this: it is for the sake of this, certainly, that we make his words our text to-day.

They are exemplified within the Church,

and without. They are exemplified in the treatment of Revelation—by believers, by doubters, by foes. The doctrine of the Trinity has been turned oftentimes, from a mystery in the Divine sense, into a mystery in the human. The soul should have calmed and hushed itself in that presence, as before the revelation of a Father, a Saviour, and a Comforter, not three Gods but one God; each Person necessary to the repose and to the activity, to the comfort and to the life, of every one of us, as we struggle along the path of difficulty into the clear light and into the perfect peace of a world in which God shall be all in all. Instead of this, speculation has been busy, and controversy has been busy, and logic has been busy, and rhetoric has been busy, and the whole matter has been referred and relegated from the tribunal of the soul to the tribunal of the intellect—theologians have exercised themselves in matters too wonderful for them—prayer has been intermitted for wrangling, and every nutritious particle has been industriously exterminated out of the bread of life.

There has been something wrong, we all say, in a process of which the result is thus disastrous. And we cannot think that the fault lay in the thoroughness or in the manifoldness of the investigation. It was not meant, we are quite sure, that any part of the man should be idle in the dealing with Revelation. Reason cannot be hostile, save by scandalous mismanagement, to that which the God of reason has spoken. Indeed, we demur altogether to the introduction into this subject of those metaphysical partitions of the unit humanity, which alone make it possible to set truth and the truth at variance, by speaking of understanding and conscience, of judgment and will, almost as of separate personalities, and drawing sharp lines between their several jurisdictions in the decision and action of the man. The man is one and but one; he moves altogether if he moves at all: and the fault lies, not in using this part of himself when he ought to have used that, but rather in the spirit in which he used either; in the forgetfulness perhaps of the necessary limitations of knowing, but still more in the posture and attitude in which he set himself to know. *My heart is not haughty, nor mine eyes lofty. I have calmed and hushed my soul.*

It may be that theologians have something to answer for in the sadder example to which we pass onward.

The life must have been secluded from common experiences—the heart must be steeled against human compassions—if the one has not known, if the other has not wept over, some shipwreck of faith of which we have here perhaps the explanation. The soul that should have 'behaved and quieted itself' has been 'exercised in great matters, in things too high for it:' and the result is that utter sweeping away of the faith and of the hope which we can speak of, in this house of God, with full assurance of sympathy, as a calamity than which there can be none greater.

There are minds—who shall gainsay it?—unqualified or disqualified for speculation. There are minds quick and shallow; capable of doubt, incapable of decision. There are minds undisciplined and uneducated, because they have not had the chance, or because they have flung the chance away. There are minds ignorant of the great gulf, fixed in reason, fixed in the nature of things, between doubting and disbelieving; minds for which the entrance of one doubt is the banishment of a million of certainties; minds destitute alike of the power to weigh and the power to number, insomuch that a sneer is as potent with them as a martyrdom, and one sentence of an infidel Magazine is answer enough and to spare to the argument of eighteen centuries of Christian lives and deaths.

To minds such as these is it not unfortunate—we say but that now—unfortunate, that the accident of the day and of the hour should have brought the suggestion of scepticism? Those of us who have seen the thing will say so; those of us who have seen the faith or seen the Ministry of Jesus Christ abandoned and flung away because the insolence of a 'Gnosis falsely so called' came across the path of a young man and told him that there can be no proof of that which you can neither touch nor taste nor smell. Would it not have been better for that intellect (so called) if it had never dabbled in speculation? Was it fit for it? Ought it not to have been differently trained—I had almost said, differently constituted—if it was ever to embark in it with advantage—by which I mean, with any prospect of finding the truth?

But these are our times, and as they are we must deal with them. It is idle to fold the hands in mournful regrettings. God has 'set the bounds of the habitation'—'Sparta is our lot, and we must adorn it." We shall enter into no comparisons, save such as breathe thankfulness, between the days that are and the days that have been. The present is a disturbing force in such calculations: we cannot stand far enough off, even in imagination, to do justice to the picture. If we were not able to counsel, neither would we complain. But the subject which we have suggested is full of admonition—for each one of us, and for all.

It is impossible to live the life of this age, and not to enquire. Close ear and eye, scepticism is in the air. It was always in books, now it is in society. A whole table was challenged lately by the question, 'Is there any one so old-fashioned as to believe the Bible?' This was an insolence, this was an outrage.

But it only exaggerated, it only distorted, a fact. On that occasion there was one man brave enough to answer, 'I do'—and the courage told. But how shall a young man in such times, educated or uneducated, exercise that calming and hushing, that behaving and quieting, which the text speaks of? Who shall prescribe the right to speculate, and the no right? Who shall lay down the conditions, present or retrospective, under which a rational being, ordained or unordained, shall be at liberty to exercise himself in great matters, too high for him or for any man? It cannot be done. And if you attempt it, you are met instantly by the cavil, Then you would leave every man in 'the tongue wherein he was born:' Mussulman, Brahmin, Buddhist, every man has his religion: if the Christian is to be kept perforce within the confines of his tradition, he must allow to others the 'protection' which is the necessity of his own.

Brethren, I speak in this place—for this once more—to a powerful phalanx of young men. You have to go forth into this outspoken, this insubordinate, this free-thinking age. If you would, you cannot alter it. You must hear its wild talk, you must move with it in its bold swing. I can desire few things better for you than that you should dread it. It is a terrible world into which you are going; terrible in its strength, terrible in its daring. This age fears nothing—neither heaven above it, nor hell beneath. It has settled for itself that the latter is not—save as an embellishment of positiveness, save as an expletive of passion. It doubts much about the former: it is more than half inclined to think that nothing is but the material. It is encouraged in these ideas by men of science, who ought to know that they themselves are moved and swayed by other forces besides the tangible. Theologians are not always consistent in their maintenance of the principle that Jesus Christ 'speaks that He doth know, and testifies that He hath seen.' They too coquet with the sceptic; offer to meet him half-way, and find, when they have done so, that he is in his cave still.

What I would presume to urge upon you, in these days of your youth, is this.

First, that you feel the responsibility of those decisions which will soon be forced upon you. Our age has one mark, I think, of a late place in the world's history, that there is a more resolute taking of sides for the great struggle; that there is less of that unmarked colourless Christianity which called Christ Lord —which counted infidelity a discourtesy and Atheism an insult—yet had no word to say when the nominal Master was either dishonoured by immorality or trodden underfoot in His brethren. This is a gain more than a loss. It makes the Gospel more real. The troops are drawing off, this way and that way, towards their positions. We are on the eve of the great battle.

We never felt, as now, the importance of Education. You have heard to-day of minds unqualified or disqualified for great matters. There is no excuse for those who, having what you have here, go forth in this state to life's battle. O, if you would learn now to thank God for your reason—to thank God for your leisure—to thank God for your books, for your lectures, for your Chapels, for your Sacraments! These are, for you, like those 'days of the Son of Man,' one of which, afterwards, you would give life to see again. How fearful, fearful for both worlds, if you should any of you go forth hence unskilled in judging between the true and the false, unable to separate between the precious and the vile, when the two present themselves, in the next stage of your being, and you must choose between them for life and death, for the life and death perhaps of more than your own soul. An educated man might almost be defined as a man who is *not soon shaken in mind, whether by word or spirit or letter*, because he has been taught by long discipline both to *prove all things* and to *hold fast that which is good*. The herd of sceptics may be *led* by an intellect—they have no intellect, generally speaking, of their own. They are at the mercy of loud talk and confident statement: it flatters while it undermines: it treats its hearers as simple, but it compliments them as wise.

Not, then, to foreclose thinking, but to prepare for it, is the work of all Education that is worth the name. And such preparation will above all things enforce that preliminary 'calming and hushing' which the text tells of. It will remind the young man that this is not the first year of the century, and not the first year of the race. It will bid him remember that he himself has a past as well as a present, and that he cannot, if he would, cut himself off from it. On any supposition it must be necessary to take into account the circumstances, over which he had no control, of his birth, of his parentage, of his nationality, of his religion. We would say it to a Mahometan, we would say it to a Hindoo. There is a presumption in favour of the thing that is. There is an antecedent probability on the side of the polity, on the side of the society, on the side of the opinion, in which you were born. To change a faith is a tremendous step: not without a moral compulsion ought it to be taken. To change from faith to no faith is a more fearful stride still : look around, above, within you— it is common prudence—ere you adventure it. These considerations are not decisive. If changes of faith were wrong, we should have no Gospel. If to leave the religion of a man's fathers were wicked, we should have no day in our Calendar for the Conversion of St Paul.

But seriousness, but awe, but reverence, but humility—these qualities are above all graces, when the question is at issue, Shall I relay my very foundations?

We will not say that there is always a want of seriousness in the scepticism of to-day. Amongst much playing at doubting, there is also a struggle and a death-grapple which is worthy of the crisis. There are men living anxious lives, there are men *standing in jeopardy every hour*, there are men dying many deaths daily, in the controversy, which they suffer no eye to watch over, between the spirit of faith and the spirit of doubting. We feel that, in the sight of Infinite Love, such men may be worthier, nobler, holier far, than the easy, complacent, conventional worshipper, whose faith stands really in the tradition of his elders, and has never been made his own by the travail of fear and grief.

None the less may there be many a grievous

error, many a deep-lying fallacy, in the process of that search. I will name two.

There are those who, so soon as a doubt enters, cease instantly to pray. They count it an insincerity to call upon Him in whom they are not certain that they believe. The memorable words, *When they saw Him, they worshipped Him, but some doubted,* are misread by them or disregarded. They do not see that to cease to worship is, not to doubt, but to cease to doubt. It is, to have settled the very question which they profess to be pondering. If there be a word of truth in the Gospel, the way of faith is the way of prayer, and the man who has ceased to call upon the God of his life is no longer so much as an enquirer whether that God has spoken to us in His Son.

There are some questions—let who will mock the saying—there are some questions which it is treason to humanity to open. Of such sort is the question of worship. The question, in other words, whether I am to myself sufficient or insufficient—whether I am to my own being the head and front, the source and spring, or certainly and at all costs an inferior, a dependent, a subject thing—impotent over the beginning, impotent over the continuance, impotent over the ending, of this unknown something which I call the life. If I knew not one word of the nature or the character or the will of the Power above me, the recognition of dependence, which is the essence of worship, would equally be my necessity, equally my duty. Better kneel to an Unknown God than kneel to nothing and to no one.

To kneel is the beauty and glory, to kneel is the truth and the hope, of the humanity that knows itself. Let the cry go forth even into the darkness—it shall 'calm and hush,' it shall 'behave and quiet,' the soul that would enquire, the soul that would know. They worshipped although—yea, they worshipped because—they doubted.

Yet one other thing. Many, when the faith is shaken, count it an insincerity to listen to any evidence but what they call the logical. They resent it as almost a fraud put upon them if any one offers the moral beauty of the Gospel, or the spiritual satisfaction to be found in it, or the cumulative force of recorded effects and consequences of believing, as furnishing, alone or all together, any argument at all in behalf of the Revelation of Jesus Christ. Intellect alone, cold, hard, dry intellect, must be the tribunal of truth. If mathematical demonstration is impossible, then, for them, it shall be impossible to believe. That conviction which the first Christian doubter made to hang upon the sight and upon the touch, they suspend upon the cogency of the Christian syllogism as it stands for the nineteenth age.

We have entered our protest against this

splitting and parcelling of the being. The man is one and but one. These separate personalities, of mind and heart, of intellect and affection, who gave them their authority and their superscription? If God speaks, He will speak, be sure, to the whole man. God is one, and the man is one—as such will he be dealt with, as such he must make reply. Intellect and heart and conscience—the power to judge, the power to admire, the power to adore—the instinct of truth, and the instinct of good, and the instinct of beauty—all these things must march as one towards the investigation of the Divine: the thing which we believe must be the satisfaction of them all, and each one must contribute its quota to the evidence and its voice to the verdict.

The counsel of the text is the counsel of wisdom, when it makes reverence, when it makes humility, the condition of all knowledge that is worth the name. It is quite possible, by a little mismanagement, by a little spoiling, of the soul, to make the spiritual life intolerable. We may so educate and so discipline our own soul, as that health shall be the reward. We may do the contrary. We may make ourselves fools, idiots, sceptics, Atheists, if we will to do so, and if we take the way.

Plain words are the most suitable to solemn subjects. This humble, this reverent estimate of our position and relationship will show itself, first of all, in a willingness to attend to small duties; to overlook nothing as beneath notice; to adapt ourselves to circumstances, mental as well as providential; to condescend (as Scripture says) to things that are lowly; to expect happiness in duty rather than in acquisition; to live the life set us, rather than to spread and stretch ourselves into an imagined universe beyond. This principle does not forbid effort—does not discourage progress—does not depress the endeavour to make the very most of every talent, and to rise to any height of honest usefulness to which the powers given may be prospered by the blessing sought. All these are indeed but the natural exercises of the composed and tranquillized spirit.

Nor is the 'refraining and quieting' spoken of inconsistent with the utmost stretch of enquiry into the mysteries of nature, of humanity, of God. This too is fostered and strengthened by it. The difference is here—that, while the man who *exercises himself in great matters,* is apt first to isolate, and then to idolize, intellect —to imagine that mental processes alone can carry him into the deep things (if there be such) of God Himself, and that whatsoever cannot be logically demonstrated cannot be certainly true; the other—not because he is afraid to seek, not because he dreads the break-down of faith under the strain of reason, but because he remembers that the being which he possesses is a complex thing, and must not be disjointed and taken to pieces in the very use of it for the highest of all conceivable purposes, the study of truth and of God—summons all and each part of himself to accompany the march, and refuses to regard that as proved, or that as disproved, which (at most) is so by one piece or one bit of him. Reason, and conscience, and heart, and soul too, shall all enter into the search, and that which satisfies not each and all of these shall not be, for him, either truth, or religion, or heaven, or God. *Knowledge puffeth up—it is love which edifieth. If any man think that he knoweth anything, he knoweth nothing yet as he ought to know.* But *if any man love God, the same* knoweth—or, let me rather say—for, after all, Divine knowledge, to be real, must be rather receptive than originative—*the same is known of God.*

I have calmed and hushed my soul, as a child weaned of his mother. Try this self-discipline, doubters in this Congregation! Set yourselves humble duties. Live much in acts of charity—domestic, social, philanthropic. Enter into lives pinched by poverty. Help boys and young men to grapple with the stern realities of want, neglect, solitude, temptation. Intellectual difficulties *must* take rank after these. Go back to their pondering a more sympathetic and therefore a wiser man. See whether some of them have not been solved by the new contact. Is not this Gospel, which looked so superfluous in the theatre and the ballroom, so assailable, by sap or storm, in the study or the lecture-room—is it not indeed the exact appliance, the very panacea, when it is brought face to face with sorrow, with bereavement, with pain, with death? Then ask yourself—ask the whole of yourself—understanding, heart, conscience, soul—whether the thing so appropriate, so strong, so beautiful, so satisfying, may not, were it but for that reason, be true.

Cambridge:
PRINTED BY C. J. CLAY, M.A.
AT THE UNIVERSITY PRESS.

BY THE SAME AUTHOR.

THE CHURCH OF THE FIRST DAYS. Lectures on the Acts of the Apostles. I. THE CHURCH OF JERUSALEM. THIRD EDITION. II. THE CHURCH OF THE GENTILES. THIRD EDITION. III. THE CHURCH OF THE WORLD. THIRD EDITION. Fcap. 8vo. 4s. 6d. each.

LECTURES ON THE REVELATION OF ST. JOHN. FOURTH EDITION. Two Vols. Extra Fcap. 8vo. 9s.

WORDS FROM THE GOSPELS. Sermons preached in the Parish Church of Doncaster. THIRD EDITION. Fcap. 8vo. 4s. 6d.

LECTURES ON THE EPISTLE TO THE PHILIPPIANS. THIRD EDITION. Crown 8vo. 7s. 6d.

TWELVE DISCOURSES on Subjects connected with the Liturgy and Worship of the Church of England. FOURTH EDITION. Fcap. 8vo. 6s.

THE BOOK AND THE LIFE: and other Sermons preached before the University of Cambridge. THIRD EDITION. Fcap. 8vo. 4s. 6d.

MEMORIALS OF HARROW SUNDAYS. A Selection of Sermons preached in Harrow School Chapel. With a View of the Chapel. FOURTH EDITION. Crown 8vo. 10s. 6d.

ST. PAUL'S EPISTLE TO THE ROMANS. The Greek Text, with English Notes. FOURTH EDITION. Crown 8vo. 7s. 6d.

LESSONS OF LIFE AND GODLINESS. A Selection of Sermons preached in the Parish Church of Doncaster. FOURTH EDITION. Fcap. 8vo. 3s. 6d.

THE EPISTLES OF ST. PAUL FOR ENGLISH READERS. Part I. containing *The First Epistle to the Thessalonians.* SECOND EDITION. 8vo. 1s. 6d.

EPIPHANY, LENT, AND EASTER. A Selection of Expository Sermons. THIRD EDITION. Crown 8vo. 10s. 6d.

LIFE'S WORK AND GOD'S DISCIPLINE. Three Sermons preached before the University of Cambridge in April and May, 1865. THIRD EDITION. Fcap. 8vo. 2s. 6d.

Macmillan and Co., London.

WORKS BY THE SAME AUTHOR—*Continued.*

THE WHOLESOME WORDS OF JESUS CHRIST.
Four Sermons preached before the University of Cambridge in November, 1866. SECOND EDITION. Fcap. 8vo. 3s. 6d.

LESSONS OF THE CROSS AND PASSION. Lectures in Hereford Cathedral during the Week before Easter, 1869. Fcap. 8vo. 2s. 6d.

FOES OF FAITH. Four Sermons preached before the University of Cambridge in November, 1868. SECOND EDITION. Fcap. 8vo. 3s. 6d.

COUNSELS FOR YOUNG STUDENTS. Three Sermons before the University of Cambridge. Fcap. 8vo. 2s. 6d.

NOTES FOR LECTURES ON CONFIRMATION. With suitable Prayers. ELEVENTH EDITION. Fcap. 8vo. 1s. 6d.

CHRIST SATISFYING THE INSTINCTS OF HUMANITY. Eight Lectures delivered in the Temple Church, Lent 1870. SECOND EDITION. Fcap. 8vo. 3s. 6d.

THE TWO GREAT TEMPTATIONS. The Temptation of Man and the Temptation of Christ. Lectures in the Temple Church, Lent 1872. SECOND EDITION. Fcap. 8vo. 3s. 6d.

WORDS FROM THE CROSS, Lent Lectures, 1875; and Thoughts for these Times, University Sermons, 1874. Extra fcap. 8vo. 4s. 6d.

THE YOUNG LIFE EQUIPPING ITSELF FOR GOD'S SERVICE. Sermons before the University of Cambridge, 1872. SIXTH EDITION. Crown 8vo. 3s. 6d.

THE SOLIDITY OF TRUE RELIGION: and other Sermons. SECOND EDITION. Extra fcap. 8vo. 3s. 6d.

FORGET THINE OWN PEOPLE: an Appeal to the Home Church for Foreign Missions. Extra fcap. 8vo. 3s. 6d.

WORDS OF HOPE FROM THE PULPIT OF THE TEMPLE CHURCH. FOURTH EDITION. Extra fcap. 8vo. 5s.

ADDRESSES TO YOUNG CLERGYMEN. Delivered at Salisbury in September and October, 1875. Extra fcap. 8vo. 4s. 6d.

HEROES OF FAITH. Lectures on Hebrews xi. Extra fcap. 8vo. 6s.

Macmillan and Co., London.

October, 1878.

A Catalogue of Theological Books, with a Short Account of their Character and Aim,

Published by

MACMILLAN AND CO.

Bedford Street, Strand, London, W.C.

Abbott (Rev. E. A.)—Works by the Rev. E. A. ABBOTT, D.D., Head Master of the City of London School:

BIBLE LESSONS. Second Edition. Crown 8vo. 4s. 6d.
"*Wise, suggestive, and really profound initiation into religious thought.*"
—Guardian. *The Bishop of St. David's, in his speech at the Education Conference at Abergwilly, says he thinks* "*nobody could read them without being the better for them himself, and being also able to see how this difficult duty of imparting a sound religious education may be effected.*"

THE GOOD VOICES: A Child's Guide to the Bible. With upwards of 50 Illustrations. Crown 8vo. cloth gilt. 5s.
"*It would not be easy to combine simplicity with fulness and depth of meaning more successfully than Mr. Abbott has done.*"—Spectator. *The Times says*—"*Mr. Abbott writes with clearness, simplicity, and the deepest religious feeling.*"

CAMBRIDGE SERMONS PREACHED BEFORE THE UNIVERSITY. Second Edition. 8vo. 6s.

ABBOTT (Rev. E. A.)—*continued.*

THROUGH NATURE TO CHRIST; or, The Ascent of Worship through Illusion to the Truth. 8vo. 12s. 6d.

"*The beauty of its style, its tender feeling, and its perfect sympathy, the originality and suggestiveness of many of its thoughts, would of themselves go far to recommend it. But far besides these, it has a certain value in its bold, comprehensive, trenchant method of apology, and in the adroitness with which it turns the flank of the many modern fallacies that caricature in order to condemn Christianity.*"—Church Quarterly Review.

Ainger (Rev. Alfred).—SERMONS PREACHED IN THE TEMPLE CHURCH. By the Rev. ALFRED AINGER, M.A. of Trinity Hall, Cambridge, Reader at the Temple Church. Extra fcap. 8vo. 6s.

"*It is,*" *the* British Quarterly *says,* "*the fresh unconventional talk of a clear independent thinker, addressed to a congregation of thinkers.... Thoughtful men will be greatly charmed by this little volume.*"

Alexander.—THE LEADING IDEAS of the GOSPELS. Five Sermons preached before the University of Oxford in 1870—71. By WILLIAM ALEXANDER, D.D., Brasenose College; Lord Bishop of Derry and Raphoe; Select Preacher. Cr. 8vo. 4s. 6d.

"*Eloquence and force of language, clearness of statement, and a hearty appreciation of the grandeur and importance of the topics upon which he writes, characterize his sermons.*"—Record.

Arnold.—Works by MATTHEW ARNOLD:

A BIBLE READING FOR SCHOOLS. THE GREAT PROPHECY OF ISRAEL'S RESTORATION (Isaiah, Chapters 40—66). Arranged and Edited for Young Learners. By MATTHEW ARNOLD, D.C.L., formerly Professor of Poetry in the University of Oxford, and Fellow of Oriel. Third Edition. 18mo. cloth. 1s.

The Times *says*—"*Whatever may be the fate of this little book in Government Schools, there can be no doubt that it will be found excellently calculated to further instruction in Biblical literature in any school into which it may be introduced.... We can safely say that whatever school uses this book, it will enable its pupils to understand Isaiah, a great advantage compared with other establishments which do not avail themselves of it.*"

ISAIAH XL.—LXVI., with the Shorter Prophecies allied to it. Arranged and Edited with Notes. Crown 8vo. 5s.

Bather.—ON SOME MINISTERIAL DUTIES, CATECHISING, PREACHING, &c. Charges by the late Archdeacon BATHER. Edited, with Preface, by Dr. C. J. VAUGHAN. Extra fcap. 8vo. 4s. 6d.

Benham.—A COMPANION TO THE LECTIONARY, being a Commentary on the Proper Lessons for Sundays and Holydays. By the Rev. W. BENHAM, B.D., Vicar of Margate. Cheaper Edition. Crown 8vo. 6s.

"*A very useful book. Mr. Benham has produced a good and welcome companion to our revised Lectionary. Its contents will, if not very original or profound, prove to be sensible and practical, and often suggestive to the preacher and the Sunday School teacher. They will also furnish some excellent Sunday reading for private hours.*"—Guardian.

Bernard.—THE PROGRESS OF DOCTRINE IN THE NEW TESTAMENT. By THOMAS D. BERNARD, M.A., Rector of Walcot and Canon of Wells. Third and Cheaper Edition. Crown 8vo. 5s. (Bampton Lectures for 1864.)

"*We lay down these lectures with a sense not only of being edified by sound teaching and careful thought, but also of being gratified by conciseness and clearness of expression and elegance of style.*"—Churchman.

Binney.—SERMONS PREACHED IN THE KING'S WEIGH HOUSE CHAPEL, 1829—69. By THOMAS BINNEY, D.D. New and Cheaper Edition. Extra fcap. 8vo. 4s. 6d.

"*Full of robust intelligence, of reverent but independent thinking on the most profound and holy themes, and of earnest practical purpose.*"—London Quarterly Review.

A SECOND SERIES OF SERMONS. Edited, with Biographical and Critical Sketch, by the Rev. HENRY ALLON, D.D. With Portrait of Dr. Binney engraved by JEENS. 8vo. 12s.

Birks.—Works by T. R. BIRKS, M.A., Professor of Moral Philosophy, Cambridge :

THE DIFFICULTIES OF BELIEF in connection with the Creation and the Fall, Redemption and Judgment. Second Edition, enlarged. Crown 8vo. 5s.

AN ESSAY ON THE RIGHT ESTIMATION OF MSS. EVIDENCE IN THE TEXT OF THE NEW TESTAMENT. Crown 8vo. 3s. 6d.

COMMENTARY ON THE BOOK OF ISAIAH, Critical, Historical and Prophetical; including a Revised English Translation. With Introduction and Appendices on the Nature of Scripture Prophecy, the Life and Times of Isaiah, the Genuineness of the Later Prophecies, the Structure and History of the whole Book, the Assyrian History in Isaiah's Days, and various Difficult Passages. Second Edition, revised. 8vo. 12s. 6d.

THEOLOGICAL BOOKS.

Bradby.—SERMONS PREACHED AT HAILEYBURY. By E. H. BRADBY, M.A., Master. 8vo. 10s. 6d.

"*He who claims a public hearing now, speaks to an audience accustomed to Cotton, Temple, Vaughan, Bradley, Butler, Farrar, and others...... Each has given us good work, several, work of rare beauty, force, or originality; but we doubt whether any one of them has touched deeper chords, or brought more freshness and strength into his sermons, than the last of their number, the present Head Master of Haileybury.*"—Spectator.

Butcher.—THE ECCLESIASTICAL CALENDAR; its Theory and Construction. By SAMUEL BUTCHER, D.D., late Bishop of Meath. 4to. 14s.

Butler (G.)—Works by the Rev. GEORGE BUTLER, M.A., Principal of Liverpool College:

FAMILY PRAYERS. Crown 8vo. 5s.

The prayers in this volume are all based on passages of Scripture—the morning prayers on Select Psalms, those for the evening on portions of the New Testament.

SERMONS PREACHED in CHELTENHAM COLLEGE CHAPEL. Crown 8vo. 7s. 6d.

Butler (Rev. H. M.)—SERMONS PREACHED in the CHAPEL OF HARROW SCHOOL. By H. MONTAGU BUTLER, Head Master. Crown 8vo. 7s. 6d.

"*These sermons are adapted for every household. There is nothing more striking than the excellent good sense with which they are imbued.*" —Spectator.

A SECOND SERIES. Crown 8vo. 7s. 6d.

"*Excellent specimens of what sermons should be—plain, direct, practical, pervaded by the true spirit of the Gospel, and holding up lofty aims before the minds of the young.*"—Athenæum.

Butler (Rev. W. Archer).—Works by the Rev. WILLIAM ARCHER BUTLER, M.A., late Professor of Moral Philosophy in the University of Dublin:

SERMONS, DOCTRINAL AND PRACTICAL. Edited, with a Memoir of the Author's Life, by THOMAS WOODWARD, Dean of Down. With Portrait. Ninth Edition. 8vo. 8s.

The Introductory Memoir narrates in considerable detail and with much interest, the events of Butler's brief life; and contains a few specimens of his poetry, and a few extracts from his addresses and essays, including a long and eloquent passage on the Province and Duty of the Preacher.

BUTLER (Rev. W. Archer)—*continued.*
  A SECOND SERIES OF SERMONS. Edited by J. A. JEREMIE, D.D., Dean of Lincoln. Seventh Edition. 8vo. 7s.
  The North British Review *says,* "*Few sermons in our language exhibit the same rare combination of excellencies; imagery almost as rich as Taylor's; oratory as vigorous often as South's; judgment as sound as Barrow's; a style as attractive but more copious, original, and forcible than Atterbury's; piety as elevated as Howe's, and a fervour as intense at times as Baxter's. Mr. Butler's are the sermons of a true poet.*"

  LETTERS ON ROMANISM, in reply to Dr. Newman's Essay on Development. Edited by the Dean of Down. Second Edition, revised by Archdeacon HARDWICK. 8vo. 10s. 6d.
  These Letters contain an exhaustive criticism of Dr. Newman's famous "Essay on the Development of Christian Doctrine." "A work which ought to be in the Library of every student of Divinity."—BP. ST. DAVID'S.

Campbell.—Works by JOHN M'LEOD CAMPBELL:
  THE NATURE OF THE ATONEMENT AND ITS RELATION TO REMISSION OF SINS AND ETERNAL LIFE. Fourth and Cheaper Edition, crown 8vo. 6s.
  "*Among the first theological treatises of this generation.*"—Guardian.
  "*One of the most remarkable theological books ever written.*"—Times.

  CHRIST THE BREAD OF LIFE. An Attempt to give a profitable direction to the present occupation of Thought with Romanism. Second Edition, greatly enlarged. Crown 8vo. 4s. 6d.
  "*Deserves the most attentive study by all who interest themselves in the predominant religious controversy of the day.*"—Spectator.

  REMINISCENCES AND REFLECTIONS, referring to his Early Ministry in the Parish of Row, 1825—31. Edited with an Introductory Narrative by his Son, DONALD CAMPBELL, M.A., Chaplain of King's College, London. Crown 8vo. 7s. 6d.
  These 'Reminiscences and Reflections,' written during the last year of his life, were mainly intended to place on record thoughts which might prove helpful to others. "*We recommend this book cordially to all who are interested in the great cause of religious reformation.*"—Times. "*There is a thoroughness and depth, as well as a practical earnestness, in his grasp of each truth on which he dilates, which make his reflections very valuable.*"—Literary Churchman.

  THOUGHTS ON REVELATION, with Special Reference to the Present Time. Second Edition. Crown 8vo. 5s.

CAMPBELL (J. M'Leod)—*continued.*

RESPONSIBILITY FOR THE GIFT OF ETERNAL LIFE. Compiled by permission of the late J. M'LEOD CAMPBELL, D.D., from Sermons preached chiefly at Row in 1829—31. Crown 8vo. *5s.*

"*There is a healthy tone as well as a deep pathos not often seen in sermons. His words are weighty and the ideas they express tend to perfection of life.*"—Westminster Review.

Campbell (Lewis).—SOME ASPECTS OF THE CHRISTIAN IDEAL. Sermons by the Rev. L. CAMPBELL, M.A., LL.D., Professor of Greek in the University of Glasgow. Crown 8vo. 6s.

Canterbury.—Works by ARCHIBALD CAMPBELL, Archbishop of Canterbury:

THE PRESENT POSITION OF THE CHURCH OF ENGLAND. Seven Addresses delivered to the Clergy and Churchwardens of his Diocese, as his Charge, at his Primary Visitation, 1872. Third Edition. 8vo. cloth. 3s. 6d.

SOME THOUGHTS ON THE DUTIES OF THE ESTABLISHED CHURCH OF ENGLAND AS A NATIONAL CHURCH. Seven Addresses delivered at his Second Visitation. 8vo. 4s. 6d.

Cheyne.—Works by T. K. CHEYNE, M.A., Fellow of Balliol College, Oxford:

THE BOOK OF ISAIAH CHRONOLOGICALLY ARRANGED. An Amended Version, with Historical and Critical Introductions and Explanatory Notes. Crown 8vo. 7s. 6d.

The Westminster Review *speaks of it as "a piece of scholarly work, very carefully and considerately done."* The Academy *calls it "a successful attempt to extend a right understanding of this important Old Testament writing."*

NOTES AND CRITICISMS on the HEBREW TEXT OF ISAIAH. Crown 8vo. 2s. 6d.

Choice Notes on the Four Gospels, drawn from Old and New Sources. Crown 8vo. 4s. 6d. each Vol. (St. Matthew and St. Mark in one Vol. price 9s.)

Church.—Works by the Very Rev. R. W. CHURCH, M.A., D.C.L., Dean of St. Paul's:

ON SOME INFLUENCES OF CHRISTIANITY UPON NATIONAL CHARACTER. Three Lectures delivered in St. Paul's Cathedral, Feb. 1873. Crown 8vo. 4s. 6d.

CHURCH (Very Rev. R. W.)—*continued.*

"*Few books that we have met with have given us keener pleasure than this....... It would be a real pleasure to quote extensively, so wise and so true, so tender and so discriminating are Dean Church's judgments, but the limits of our space are inexorable. We hope the book will be bought.*"
—Literary Churchman.

THE SACRED POETRY OF EARLY RELIGIONS. Two Lectures in St. Paul's Cathedral. 18mo. 1s. I. The Vedas. II. The Psalms.

ST. ANSELM. Second Edition. Crown 8vo. 6s.

"*It is a sketch by the hand of a master, with every line marked by taste, learning, and real apprehension of the subject.*"—Pall Mall Gazette.

HUMAN LIFE AND ITS CONDITIONS. Sermons preached before the University of Oxford, 1876—78, with Three Ordination Sermons. Crown 8vo. 6s.

Clergyman's Self-Examination concerning the APOSTLES' CREED. Extra fcap. 8vo. 1s. 6d.

Colenso.—THE COMMUNION SERVICE FROM THE BOOK OF COMMON PRAYER; with Select Readings from the Writings of the Rev. F. D. MAURICE, M.A. Edited by the Right Rev. J. W. COLENSO, D.D., Lord Bishop of Natal. New Edition. 16mo. 2s. 6d.

Collects of the Church of England. With a beautifully Coloured Floral Design to each Collect, and Illuminated Cover. Crown 8vo. 12s. Also kept in various styles of morocco.

The distinctive characteristic of this edition is the coloured floral design which accompanies each Collect, and which is generally emblematical of the character of the day or saint to which it is assigned; the flowers which have been selected are such as are likely to be in bloom on the day to which the Collect belongs. The Guardian *thinks it* "*a successful attempt to associate in a natural and unforced manner the flowers of our fields and gardens with the course of the Christian year.*"

Congreve.—HIGH HOPES, AND PLEADINGS FOR A REASONABLE FAITH, NOBLER THOUGHTS, LARGER CHARITY. Sermons preached in the Parish Church of Tooting Graveney, Surrey. By J. CONGREVE, M.A., Rector. Cheaper Issue. Crown 8vo. 5s.

Cotton.—Works by the late GEORGE EDWARD LYNCH COTTON, D.D., Bishop of Calcutta :

COTTON (Bishop)—*continued.*

SERMONS PREACHED TO ENGLISH CONGREGATIONS IN INDIA. Crown 8vo. 7s. 6d.

EXPOSITORY SERMONS ON THE EPISTLES FOR THE SUNDAYS OF THE CHRISTIAN YEAR. Two Vols. Crown 8vo. 15s.

Curteis.—DISSENT in its RELATION to the CHURCH OF ENGLAND. Eight Lectures preached before the University of Oxford, in the year 1871, on the foundation of the late Rev. John Bampton, M.A., Canon of Salisbury. By GEORGE HERBERT CURTEIS, M.A., late Fellow and Sub-Rector of Exeter College; Principal of the Lichfield Theological College, and Prebendary of Lichfield Cathedral; Rector of Turweston, Bucks. New Edition. Crown 8vo. 7s. 6d.

"*Mr. Curteis has done good service by maintaining in an eloquent, temperate, and practical manner, that discussion among Christians is really an evil, and that an intelligent basis can be found for at least a proximate union.*"—Saturday Review. "*A well timed, learned, and thoughtful book.*"

Davies.—Works by the Rev. J. LLEWELYN DAVIES, M.A., Rector of Christ Church, St. Marylebone, etc. :

THE GOSPEL AND MODERN LIFE; with a Preface on a Recent Phase of Deism. Second Edition. To which is added Morality according to the Sacrament of the Lord's Supper, or Three Discourses on the Names Eucharist, Sacrifice, and Communion. Extra fcap. 8vo. 6s.

WARNINGS AGAINST SUPERSTITION IN FOUR SERMONS FOR THE DAY. Extra fcap. 8vo. 2s. 6d.

"*We have seldom read a wiser little book. The Sermons are short, terse, and full of true spiritual wisdom, expressed with a lucidity and a moderation that must give them weight even with those who agree least with their author....... Of the volume as a whole it is hardly possible to speak with too cordial an appreciation.*"—Spectator.

THE CHRISTIAN CALLING. Sermons. Extra fcap. 8vo. 6s.

Donaldson.—THE APOSTOLICAL FATHERS: a Critical Account of their Genuine Writings and of their Doctrines. By JAMES DONALDSON, LL.D. Crown 8vo. 7s. 6d.

DONALDSON (J., LL.D.)—*continued.*

This book was published in 1864 as the first volume of a 'Critical History of Christian Literature and Doctrine from the death of the Apostles to the Nicene Council.' The intention was to carry down the history continuously to the time of Eusebius, and this intention has not been abandoned. But as the writers can be sometimes grouped more easily according to subject or locality than according to time, it is deemed advisable to publish the history of each group separately. The Introduction to the present volume serves as an introduction to the whole period.

Drake.—THE TEACHING OF THE CHURCH DURING THE FIRST THREE CENTURIES ON THE DOCTRINES OF THE CHRISTIAN PRIESTHOOD AND SACRIFICE. By the Rev. C. B. DRAKE, M.A., Warden of the Church of England Hall, Manchester. Crown 8vo. 4s. 6d.

Eadie.—Works by JOHN EADIE, D.D., LL.D., Professor of Biblical Literature and Exegesis, United Presbyterian Church:

THE ENGLISH BIBLE. An External and Critical History of the various English Translations of Scripture, with Remarks on the Need of Revising the English New Testament. Two vols. 8vo. 28s.

"Accurate, scholarly, full of completest sympathy with the translators and their work, and marvellously interesting."—Literary Churchman.

"The work is a very valuable one. It is the result of vast labour, sound scholarship, and large erudition."—British Quarterly Review.

ST. PAUL'S EPISTLES TO THE THESSALONIANS. A Commentary on the Greek Text. Edited by the Rev. W. YOUNG, M.A., with a Preface by the Rev. Professor CAIRNS, D.D. 8vo. 12s.

Ecce Homo. A SURVEY OF THE LIFE AND WORK OF JESUS CHRIST. Fourteenth Edition. Crown 8vo. 6s.

"A very original and remarkable book, full of striking thought and delicate perception; a book which has realised with wonderful vigour and freshness the historical magnitude of Christ's work, and which here and there gives us readings of the finest kind of the probable motive of His individual words and actions."—Spectator. *"The best and most established believer will find it adding some fresh buttresses to his faith."*—Literary Churchman. *"If we have not misunderstood him, we have before us a writer who has a right to claim deference from those who think deepest and know most."*—Guardian.

Faber.—SERMONS AT A NEW SCHOOL. By the Rev. ARTHUR FABER, M.A., Head Master of Malvern College. Cr. 8vo. 6s.

"*These are high-toned, earnest Sermons, orthodox and scholarlike, and laden with encouragement and warning, wisely adapted to the needs of school-life.*"—Literary Churchman.

Farrar.—Works by the Rev. F. W. FARRAR, D.D., F.R.S., Canon of Westminster, late Head Master of Marlborough College:

THE FALL OF MAN, AND OTHER SERMONS. Third Edition. Crown 8vo. 6s.

The Nonconformist says of these Sermons, "Mr. Farrar's Sermons are almost perfect specimens of one type of Sermons, which we may concisely call beautiful. The style of expression is beautiful—there is beauty in the thoughts, the illustrations, the allusions—they are expressive of genuinely beautiful perceptions and feelings." The British Quarterly *says, "Ability, eloquence, scholarship, and practical usefulness, are in these Sermons combined in a very unusual degree."*

THE WITNESS OF HISTORY TO CHRIST. Being the Hulsean Lectures for 1870. Fourth Edition. Crown 8vo. 5s.

The following are the subjects of the Five Lectures:—I. "The Antecedent Credibility of the Miraculous." II. "The Adequacy of the Gospel Records." III. "The Victories of Christianity." IV. "Christianity and the Individual." V. "Christianity and the Race." The subjects of the four Appendices are:—A. "The Diversity of Christian Evidences." B. "Confucius." C. "Buddha." D. "Comte."

SEEKERS AFTER GOD. The Lives of Seneca, Epictetus, and Marcus Aurelius. New Edition. Crown 8vo. 6s.

"*A very interesting and valuable book.*"—Saturday Review.

THE SILENCE AND VOICES OF GOD: University and other Sermons. Third Edition. Crown 8vo. 6s.

"*We can most cordially recommend Dr. Farrar's singularly beautiful volume of Sermons...... For beauty of diction, felicity of style, aptness of illustration and earnest loving exhortation, the volume is without its parallel.*"—John Bull. "*They are marked by great ability, by an honesty which does not hesitate to acknowledge difficulties and by an earnestness which commands respect.*"—Pall Mall Gazette.

"IN THE DAYS OF THY YOUTH." Sermons on Practical Subjects, preached at Marlborough College from 1871—76. Third Edition. Crown 8vo. 9s.

FARRAR (Rev. F. W.)—*continued.*

"All Dr. Farrar's peculiar charm of style is apparent here, all that care and subtleness of analysis, and an even-added distinctness and clearness of moral teaching, which is what every kind of sermon wants, and especially a sermon to boys."—Literary Churchman.

>ETERNAL HOPE. Five Sermons preached in Westminster Abbey, in 1876. With Preface, Notes, etc. Contents : What Heaven is.—Is Life Worth Living?—'Hell,' What it is not.—Are there few that be saved?—Earthly and Future Consequences of Sin. Ninth Thousand. Crown 8vo. 6s.

>SAINTLY WORKERS. Lenten Lectures delivered in St. Andrew's, Holborn, March and April, 1878. Crown 8vo. 6s.

Fellowship : LETTERS ADDRESSED TO MY SISTER MOURNERS. Fcap. 8vo. cloth gilt. 3s. 6d.

Ferrar.—A COLLECTION OF FOUR IMPORTANT MSS. OF THE GOSPELS, viz., 13, 69, 124, 346, with a view to prove their common origin, and to restore the Text of their Archetype. By the late W. H. FERRAR, M.A., Professor of Latin in the University of Dublin. Edited by T. K. ABBOTT, M.A., Professor of Biblical Greek, Dublin. 4to., half morocco. 10s. 6d.

Forbes.—THE VOICE OF GOD IN THE PSALMS. By GRANVILLE FORBES, Rector of Broughton. Cr. 8vo. 6s. 6d.

Hardwick.—Works by the Ven. ARCHDEACON HARDWICK :

>CHRIST AND OTHER MASTERS. A Historical Inquiry into some of the Chief Parallelisms and Contrasts between Christianity and the Religious Systems of the Ancient World. New Edition, revised, and a Prefatory Memoir by the Rev. FRANCIS PROCTER, M.A. Fourth and Cheaper Edition. Cr. 8vo. 10s. 6d.

The plan of the work is boldly and almost nobly conceived. . . . We commend it to the perusal of all those who take interest in the study of ancient mythology, without losing their reverence for the supreme authority of the oracles of the living God."—Christian Observer.

>A HISTORY OF THE CHRISTIAN CHURCH. Middle Age. From Gregory the Great to the Excommunication of Luther, Edited by WILLIAM STUBBS, M.A., Regius Professor of Modern History in the University of Oxford. With Four Maps constructed for this work by A. KEITH JOHNSTON. Fourth Edition. Crown 8vo. 10s. 6d.

HARDWICK (Ven. Archdeacon)—*continued.*

"*As a Manual for the student of ecclesiastical history in the Middle Ages, we know no English work which can be compared to Mr. Hardwick's book.*"—Guardian.

A HISTORY of the CHRISTIAN CHURCH DURING THE REFORMATION. Fifth Edition, revised by Professor STUBBS. Crown 8vo. 10s. 6d.

This volume is intended as a sequel and companion to the "History of the Christian Church during the Middle Age."

Hare.—Works by the late ARCHDEACON HARE:

THE VICTORY OF FAITH. By JULIUS CHARLES HARE, M.A., Archdeacon of Lewes. Edited by Prof. PLUMPTRE. With Introductory Notices by the late Prof. MAURICE and Dean STANLEY. Third Edition. Crown 8vo. 6s. 6d.

THE MISSION OF THE COMFORTER. With Notes. New Edition, edited by Prof. E. H. PLUMPTRE. Crn. 8vo. 7s. 6d.

Harris.—SERMONS. By the late GEORGE COLLYER HARRIS, Prebendary of Exeter, and Vicar of St. Luke's, Torquay. With Memoir by CHARLOTTE M. YONGE, and Portrait. Extra fcap. 8vo. 6s.

Hervey.—THE GENEALOGIES OF OUR LORD AND SAVIOUR JESUS CHRIST, as contained in the Gospels of St. Matthew and St. Luke, reconciled with each other, and shown to be in harmony with the true Chronology of the Times. By Lord ARTHUR HERVEY, Bishop of Bath and Wells. 8vo. 10s. 6d.

Hort.—TWO DISSERTATIONS. I. On ΜΟΝΟΓΕΝΗΣ ΘΕΟΣ in Scripture and Tradition. II. On the "Constantinopolitan" Creed and other Eastern Creeds of the Fourth Century. By F. J. A. HORT, D.D., Fellow and Divinity Lecturer of Emmanuel College, Cambridge. 8vo. 7s. 6d.

Howson (Dean)—Works by:

BEFORE THE TABLE. An Inquiry, Historical and Theological, into the True Meaning of the Consecration Rubric in the Communion Service of the Church of England. By the Very Rev. J. S. HOWSON, D.D., Dean of Chester. With an Appendix and Supplement containing Papers by the Right Rev. the Bishop of St. Andrew's and the Rev. R. W. KENNION, M.A. 8vo. 7s. 6d.

HOWSON (Dean)—*continued.*

THE POSITION OF THE PRIEST DURING CONSECRATION IN THE ENGLISH COMMUNION SERVICE. A Supplement and a Reply. Crown 8vo. 2s. 6d.

Hymni Ecclesiæ.—Fcap. 8vo. 7s. 6d.

This collection was edited by Dr. Newman while he lived at Oxford.

Hyacinthe.—CATHOLIC REFORM. By FATHER HYACINTHE. Letters, Fragments, Discourses. Translated by Madame HYACINTHE-LOYSON. With a Preface by the Very Rev. A. P. STANLEY, D.D., Dean of Westminster. Cr. 8vo. 7s. 6d.

"*A valuable contribution to the religious literature of the day, and is especially opportune at a time when a controversy of no ordinary importance upon the very subject it deals with is engaged in all over Europe.*"—Daily Telegraph.

Imitation of Christ.—FOUR BOOKS. Translated from the Latin, with Preface by the Rev. W. BENHAM, B.D., Vicar of Margate. Printed with Borders in the Ancient Style after Holbein, Dürer, and other Old Masters. Containing Dances of Death, Acts of Mercy, Emblems, and a variety of curious ornamentation. Cr. 8vo. gilt edges. 7s. 6d.

Jacob.—BUILDING IN SCIENCE, AND OTHER SERMONS. By J. A. JACOB, M.A., Minister of St. Thomas's, Paddington. Extra fcap. 8vo. 6s.

Jennings and Lowe.—THE PSALMS, with Introductions and Critical Notes. By A. C. JENNINGS, B.A., Jesus College, Cambridge, Tyrwhitt Scholar, Crosse Scholar, Hebrew University Scholar, and Fry Scholar of St. John's College; helped in parts by W. H. LOWE, M.A., Hebrew Lecturer and late Scholar of Christ's College, Cambridge, and Tyrwhitt Scholar. Complete in two vols. crown 8vo. 10s. 6d. each. Vol. 1, Psalms i.—lxxii., with Prolegomena; Vol. 2, Psalms lxxiii.—cl.

Killen.—THE ECCLESIASTICAL HISTORY OF IRELAND from the Earliest Period to the Present Time. By W. D. KILLEN, D.D., President of Assembly's College, Belfast, and Professor of Ecclesiastical History. Two vols. 8vo. 25s.

"*Those who have the leisure will do well to read these two volumes. They are full of interest, and are the result of great research.*"—Spectator.

Kingsley.—Works by the late Rev. CHARLES KINGSLEY, M.A., Rector of Eversley, and Canon of Westminster:

THE WATER OF LIFE, AND OTHER SERMONS. Fourth Edition. Fcap. 8vo. 3s. 6d.

THE GOSPEL OF THE PENTATEUCH; AND DAVID. New Edition. Crown. 8vo. 6s.

GOOD NEWS OF GOD. Eighth Edition. Crown 8vo. 6s.

SERMONS FOR THE TIMES. Third Edition. Fcap. 8vo. 3s. 6d.

VILLAGE AND TOWN AND COUNTRY SERMONS. New Edition. Crown 8vo. 6s.

SERMONS on NATIONAL SUBJECTS. Second Edition. Fcap. 8vo. 3s. 6d.

THE KING OF THE EARTH, and other Sermons, a Second Series of Sermons on National Subjects. Second Edition. Fcap. 8vo. 3s. 6d.

DISCIPLINE, AND OTHER SERMONS. Second Edition. Fcap. 8vo. 3s. 6d.

The Guardian *says,—"There is much thought, tenderness, and devoutness of spirit in these Sermons, and some of them are models both in matter and expression."*

WESTMINSTER SERMONS. With Preface. New and Cheaper Edition. Crown 8vo. 6s.

Kynaston.—SERMONS PREACHED IN THE COLLEGE CHAPEL, CHELTENHAM, during the First Year of his Office. By the Rev. HERBERT KYNASTON, M.A., Principal of Cheltenham College. Crown 8vo. 6s.

Lightfoot.—Works by J. B. LIGHTFOOT, D.D., Hulsean Professor of Divinity in the University of Cambridge; Canon of St. Paul's:

S. PAUL'S EPISTLE TO THE GALATIANS. A Revised Text, with Introduction, Notes, and Dissertations. Fifth Edition, revised. 8vo. cloth. 12s.

While the Author's object has been to make this commentary generally

LIGHTFOOT (Rev. J. B.)—*continued.*

complete, he has paid special attention to everything relating to St. Paul's personal history and his intercourse with the Apostles and Church of the Circumcision, as it is this feature in the Epistle to the Galatians which has given it an overwhelming interest in recent theological controversy. The Spectator *says*, "*There is no commentator at once of sounder judgment and more liberal than Dr. Lightfoot.*"

> ST. PAUL'S EPISTLE TO THE PHILIPPIANS. A Revised Text, with Introduction, Notes, and Dissertations. Fourth Edition, revised. 8vo. 12s.

"*No commentary in the English language can be compared with it in regard to fulness of information, exact scholarship, and laboured attempts to settle everything about the epistle on a solid foundation.*"—Athenæum.

> ST. PAUL'S EPISTLES TO THE COLOSSIANS AND PHILEMON. A Revised Text with Introduction, Notes, etc. Second Edition. 8vo. 12s.

"*It bears marks of continued and extended reading and research, and of ampler materials at command. Indeed, it leaves nothing to be desired by those who seek to study thoroughly the epistles contained in it, and to do so with all known advantages presented in sufficient detail and in convenient form.*"—Guardian.

> S. CLEMENT OF ROME, THE TWO EPISTLES TO THE CORINTHIANS. A Revised Text, with Introduction and Notes. 8vo. 8s. 6d.

This volume is the first part of a complete edition of the Apostolic Fathers. The Introductions deal with the questions of the genuineness and authenticity of the Epistles, discuss their date and character, and analyse their contents. An account is also given of all the different epistles which bear the name of Clement of Rome. "*By far the most copiously annotated edition of St. Clement which we yet possess, and the most convenient in every way for the English reader.*"—Guardian.

> S. CLEMENT OF ROME. An Appendix containing the newly discovered portions of the two Epistles to the Corinthians with Introductions and Notes, and a Translation of the whole. 8vo. 8s. 6d.

> ON A FRESH REVISION OF THE ENGLISH NEW TESTAMENT. Second Edition. Crown 8vo. 6s.

The Author shews in detail the necessity for a fresh revision of the authorized version on the following grounds:—1. False Readings. 2. Artificial distinctions created. 3. Real distinctions obliterated. 4. Faults *of Grammar.* 5. *Faults of Lexicography.* 6. *Treatment of Proper Names, official titles, etc.* 7. *Archaisms, defects in the English, errors of the press, etc.* "*The book is marked by careful scholarship, familiarity with the subject, sobriety, and circumspection.*"—Athenæum.

Lorne.—THE PSALMS LITERALLY RENDERED IN VERSE. By the MARQUIS OF LORNE. With three Illustrations. New Edition. Crown 8vo. 7s. 6d.

Luckock.—THE TABLES OF STONE. A Course of Sermons preached in All Saints' Church, Cambridge, by H. M. LUCKOCK, M.A., Canon of Ely. Fcap. 8vo. 3s. 6d.

Maclaren.—SERMONS PREACHED at MANCHESTER. By ALEXANDER MACLAREN. Sixth Edition. Fcap. 8vo. 4s. 6d.

These Sermons represent no special school, but deal with the broad principles of Christian truth, especially in their bearing on practical, every day life. A few of the titles are:—"*The Stone of Stumbling,*" "*Love and Forgiveness,*" "*The Living Dead,*" "*Memory in Another World,*" "*Faith in Christ,*" "*Love and Fear,*" "*The Choice of Wisdom,*" "*The Food of the World.*"

A SECOND SERIES OF SERMONS. Fourth Edition. Fcap. 8vo. 4s. 6d.

The Spectator *characterises them as* "*vigorous in style, full of thought, rich in illustration, and in an unusual degree interesting.*"

A THIRD SERIES OF SERMONS. Third Edition. Fcap. 8vo. 4s. 6d.

"*Sermons more sober and yet more forcible, and with a certain wise and practical spirituality about them it would not be easy to find.*"—Spectator.

WEEK-DAY EVENING ADDRESSES. Delivered in Manchester. Extra Fcap. 8vo. 2s. 6d.

Maclear.—Works by the Rev. G. F. MACLEAR, D.D., Head Master of King's College School:

A CLASS-BOOK OF OLD TESTAMENT HISTORY. With Four Maps. New Edition. 18mo. 4s. 6d.

"*The present volume,*" *says the Preface,* "*forms a Class-Book of Old Testament History from the Earliest Times to those of Ezra and Nehemiah. In its preparation the most recent authorities have been consulted, and wherever it has appeared useful, Notes have been subjoined illustrative of the Text, and, for the sake of more advanced students, references*

MACLEAR (Dr. G. F.)—*continued.*

added to larger works. The Index has been so arranged as to form a concise Dictionary of the Persons and Places mentioned in the course of the Narrative." The Maps, prepared by Stanford, materially add to the value and usefulness of the book. The British Quarterly Review *calls it " A careful and elaborate, though brief compendium of all that modern research has done for the illustration of the Old Testament. We know of no work which contains so much important information in so small a compass."*

A CLASS-BOOK OF NEW TESTAMENT HISTORY.
Including the Connexion of the Old and New Testament. New Edition. 18mo. 5s. 6d.

The present volume forms a sequel to the Author's Class-Book of Old Testament History, and continues the narrative to the close of S. Paul's second imprisonment at Rome. The work is divided into three Books— I. The Connection between the Old and New Testament. II. The Gospel History. III. The Apostolic History. In the Appendix are given Chronological Tables. The Clerical Journal *says, " It is not often that such an amount of useful and interesting matter on biblical subjects, is found in so convenient and small a compass, as in this well-arranged volume."*

A CLASS-BOOK OF THE CATECHISM OF THE CHURCH OF ENGLAND. New and Cheaper Edition. 18mo. 1s. 6d.

The present work is intended as a sequel to the two preceding books. " Like them, it is furnished with notes and references to larger works, and it is hoped that it may be found, especially in the higher forms of our Public Schools, to supply a suitable manual of instruction in the chief doctrines of our Church, and a useful help in the preparation of Candidates for Confirmation." The Literary Churchman *says, " It is indeed the work of a scholar and divine, and as such, though extremely simple, it is also extremely instructive. There are few clergy who would not find it useful in preparing candidates for Confirmation; and there are not a few who would find it useful to themselves as well."*

A FIRST CLASS-BOOK OF THE CATECHISM OF THE CHURCH OF ENGLAND, with Scripture Proofs for Junior Classes and Schools. New Edition. 18mo. 6d.

This is an epitome of the larger Class-book, meant for junior students and elementary classes. The book has been carefully condensed, so as to contain clearly and fully, the most important part of the contents of the larger book.

MACLEAR (Dr. G. F.)—*continued.*

A SHILLING-BOOK of OLD TESTAMENT HISTORY. New Edition. 18mo. cloth limp. 1s.

This Manual bears the same relation to the larger Old Testament History, that the book just mentioned does to the larger work on the Catechism. It consists of Ten Books, divided into short chapters, and subdivided into sections, each section treating of a single episode in the history, the title of which is given in bold type.

A SHILLING-BOOK of NEW TESTAMENT HISTORY. New Edition. 18mo. cloth limp. 1s.

A MANUAL OF INSTRUCTION FOR CONFIRMATION AND FIRST COMMUNION, with Prayers and Devotions. 32mo. cloth extra, red edges. 2s.

This is an enlarged and improved edition of 'The Order of Confirmation.' To it have been added the Communion Office, with Notes and Explanations, together with a brief form of Self Examination and Devotions selected from the works of Cosin, Ken, Wilson, and others.

THE ORDER OF CONFIRMATION, with Prayers and Devotions. 32mo. cloth. 6d.

THE FIRST COMMUNION, with Prayers and Devotions for the Newly Confirmed. 32mo. 6d.

THE HOUR OF SORROW; or, The Order for the Burial of the Dead. With Prayers and Hymns. 32mo. cloth extra. 2s.

APOSTLES OF MEDIÆVAL EUROPE. Cr. 8vo. 4s. 6d.

In two Introductory Chapters the author notices some of the chief characteristics of the mediæval period itself; gives a graphic sketch of the devastated state of Europe at the beginning of that period, and an interesting account of the religions of the three great groups of vigorous barbarians— the Celts, the Teutons, and the Sclaves—who had, wave after wave, overflowed its surface. He then proceeds to sketch the lives and work of the chief of the courageous men who devoted themselves to the stupendous task of their conversion and civilization, during a period extending from the 5th to the 13th century; such as St. Patrick, St. Columba, St. Columbanus, St. Augustine of Canterbury, St. Boniface, St. Olaf, St. Cyril, Raymond Sull, and others. "Mr. Maclear will have done a great work if his admirable little volume shall help to break up the dense ignorance which is still prevailing among people at large."—Literary Churchman.

Macmillan.—Works by the Rev. HUGH MACMILLAN, LL.D., F.R.S.E. (For other Works by the same Author, see CATALOGUE OF TRAVELS and SCIENTIFIC CATALOGUE).

MACMILLAN (Rev. H., LL.D.)—*continued.*

THE TRUE VINE; or, the Analogies of our Lord's Allegory. Third Edition. Globe 8vo. 6s.

The Nonconformist *says,* "*It abounds in exquisite bits of description, and in striking facts clearly stated.*" *The* British Quarterly *says,* "*Readers and preachers who are unscientific will find many of his illustrations as valuable as they are beautiful.*"

BIBLE TEACHINGS IN NATURE. Twelfth Edition. Globe 8vo. 6s.

In this volume the author has endeavoured to shew that the teaching of Nature and the teaching of the Bible are directed to the same great end; that the Bible contains the spiritual truths which are necessary to make us wise unto salvation, and the objects and scenes of Nature are the pictures by which these truths are illustrated. "*He has made the world more beautiful to us, and unsealed our ears to voices of praise and messages of love that might otherwise have been unheard.*"—British Quarterly Review. "*Mr. Macmillan has produced a book which may be fitly described as one of the happiest efforts for enlisting physical science in the direct service of religion.*"—Guardian.

THE SABBATH OF THE FIELDS. A Sequel to "Bible Teachings in Nature." Second Edition. Globe 8vo. 6s.

"*This volume, like all Dr. Macmillan's productions, is very delightful reading, and of a special kind. Imagination, natural science, and religious instruction are blended together in a very charming way.*"—British Quarterly Review.

THE MINISTRY OF NATURE. Fourth Edition. Globe 8vo. 6s.

"*Whether the reader agree or not with his conclusions, he will acknowledge he is in the presence of an original and thoughtful writer.*"—Pall Mall Gazette. "*There is no class of educated men and women that will not profit by these essays.*"—Standard.

OUR LORD'S THREE RAISINGS FROM THE DEAD. Globe 8vo. 6s.

M'Clellan.—THE NEW TESTAMENT. A New Translation on the Basis of the Authorised Version, from a Critically revised Greek Text, with Analyses, copious References and Illustrations from original authorities, New Chronological and Analytical Harmony of the Four Gospels, Notes and Dissertations. A contribution to Christian Evidence. By JOHN BROWN M'CLELLAN, M.A., late Fellow of Trinity College, Cambridge. In Two

M'CLELLAN (J. B.)—*continued.*

Vols. Vol. I.—The Four Gospels with the Chronological and Analytical Harmony. 8vo. 30s.

"*One of the most remarkable productions of recent times,*" *says the* Theological Review, "*in this department of sacred literature;*" *and the* British Quarterly Review *terms it* "*a thesaurus of first-hand investigations.*" "*Of singular excellence, and sure to make its mark on the criticism of the New Testament.*"—John Bull.

Maurice.—Works by the late Rev. F. DENISON MAURICE, M.A., Professor of Moral Philosophy in the University of Cambridge:

The Spectator *says,*—"*Few of those of our own generation whose names will live in English history or literature have exerted so profound and so permanent an influence as Mr. Maurice.*"

THE PATRIARCHS AND LAWGIVERS OF THE OLD TESTAMENT. Third and Cheaper Edition. Crown 8vo. 5s.

The Nineteen Discourses contained in this volume were preached in the chapel of Lincoln's Inn during the year 1851. *The texts are taken from the books of Genesis, Exodus, Numbers, Deuteronomy, Joshua, Judges, and Samuel, and involve some of the most interesting biblical topics discussed in recent times.*

THE PROPHETS AND KINGS OF THE OLD TESTAMENT. Third Edition, with new Preface. Crown 8vo. 10s. 6d.

Mr. Maurice, in the spirit which animated the compilers of the Church Lessons, has in these Sermons regarded the Prophets more as preachers of righteousness than as mere predictors—an aspect of their lives which, he thinks, has been greatly overlooked in our day, and than which, there is none we have more need to contemplate. He has found that the Old Testament Prophets, taken in their simple natural sense, clear up many of the difficulties which beset us in the daily work of life; make the past intelligible, the present endurable, and the future real and hopeful.

THE GOSPEL OF THE KINGDOM OF HEAVEN. A Series of Lectures on the Gospel of St. Luke. Crown 8vo. 9s.

Mr. Maurice, in his Preface to these Twenty-eight Lectures, says,— "*In these Lectures I have endeavoured to ascertain what is told us respecting the life of Jesus by one of those Evangelists who proclaim Him to be the Christ, who says that He did come from a Father, that He did baptize with the Holy Spirit, that He did rise from the dead. I have chosen the*

MAURICE (Rev. F. D.)—*continued.*

one who is most directly connected with the later history of the Church, who was not an Apostle, who professedly wrote for the use of a man already instructed in the faith of the Apostles. I have followed the course of the writer's narrative, not changing it under any pretext. I have adhered to his phraseology, striving to avoid the substitution of any other for his."

THE GOSPEL OF ST. JOHN. A Series of Discourses.
Third and Cheaper Edition. Crown 8vo. 6s.

The Literary Churchman *thus speaks of this volume:* "*Thorough honesty, reverence, and deep thought pervade the work, which is every way solid and philosophical, as well as theological, and abounding with suggestions which the patient student may draw out more at length for himself.*"

THE EPISTLES OF ST. JOHN. A Series of Lectures
on Christian Ethics. Second and Cheaper Edition. Cr. 8vo. 6s.

These Lectures on Christian Ethics were delivered to the students of the Working Men's College, Great Ormond Street, London, on a series of Sunday mornings. Mr. Maurice believes that the question in which we are most interested, the question which most affects our studies and our daily lives, is the question, whether there is a foundation for human morality, or whether it is dependent upon the opinions and fashions of different ages and countries. This important question will be found amply and fairly discussed in this volume, which the National Review *calls* "*Mr. Maurice's most effective and instructive work. He is peculiarly fitted by the constitution of his mind, to throw light on St. John's writings.*" *Appended is a note on* "*Positivism and its Teacher.*"

EXPOSITORY SERMONS ON THE PRAYER-BOOK.
The Prayer-book considered especially in reference to the Romish System. Second Edition. Fcap. 8vo. 5s. 6d.

After an Introductory Sermon, Mr. Maurice goes over the various parts of the Church Service, expounds in eighteen Sermons, their intention and significance, and shews how appropriate they are as expressions of the deepest longings and wants of all classes of men.

WHAT IS REVELATION? A Series of Sermons on the
Epiphany; to which are added, Letters to a Theological Student on the Bampton Lectures of Mr. Mansel. Crown 8vo. 10s. 6d.

Both Sermons and Letters were called forth by the doctrine maintained by Mr. Mansel in his Bampton Lectures, that Revelation cannot be a direct Manifestation of the Infinite Nature of God. Mr. Maurice maintains

MAURICE (Rev. F. D.)—*continued.*

the opposite doctrine, and in his Sermons explains why, in spite of the high authorities on the other side, he must still assert the principle which he discovers in the Services of the Church and throughout the Bible.

SEQUEL TO THE INQUIRY, "WHAT IS REVELATION?" Letters in Reply to Mr. Mansel's Examination of "Strictures on the Bampton Lectures." Crown 8vo. 6s.

This, as the title indicates, was called forth by Mr. Mansel's Examination of Mr. Maurice's Strictures on his doctrine of the Infinite.

THEOLOGICAL ESSAYS. Third Edition. Crown 8vo. 10s. 6d.

"The book," says Mr. Maurice, "expresses thoughts which have been working in my mind for years; the method of it has not been adopted carelessly; even the composition has undergone frequent revision." There are seventeen Essays in all, and although meant primarily for Unitarians, to quote the words of the Clerical Journal, *"it leaves untouched scarcely any topic which is in agitation in the religious world; scarcely a moot point between our various sects; scarcely a plot of debateable ground between Christians and Infidels, between Romanists and Protestants, between Socinians and other Christians, between English Churchmen and Dissenters on both sides. Scarce is there a misgiving, a difficulty, an aspiration stirring amongst us now—now, when men seem in earnest as hardly ever before about religion, and ask and demand satisfaction with a fearlessness which seems almost awful when one thinks what is at stake—which is not recognised and grappled with by Mr. Maurice."*

THE DOCTRINE OF SACRIFICE DEDUCED FROM THE SCRIPTURES. Crown 8vo. 7s. 6d.

THE RELIGIONS OF THE WORLD, AND THEIR RELATIONS TO CHRISTIANITY. Fifth Edition. Crown 8vo. 5s.

ON THE LORD'S PRAYER. Fourth Edition. Fcap. 8vo. 2s. 6d.

ON THE SABBATH DAY; the Character of the Warrior, and on the Interpretation of History. Fcap. 8vo. 2s. 6d.

THE LORD'S PRAYER, THE CREED, AND THE COMMANDMENTS. A Manual for Parents and Schoolmasters. To which is added the Order of the Scriptures. 18mo. cloth limp. 1s.

DIALOGUES ON FAMILY WORSHIP. Crown 8vo. 6s.

THEOLOGICAL BOOKS.

MAURICE (Rev. F. D.)—*continued.*

SOCIAL MORALITY. Twenty-one Lectures delivered in the University of Cambridge. New and Cheaper Edition. Cr. 8vo. 10s. 6d.

"*Whilst reading it we are charmed by the freedom from exclusiveness and prejudice, the large charity, the loftiness of thought, the eagerness to recognise and appreciate whatever there is of real worth extant in the world, which animates it from one end to the other. We gain new thoughts and new ways of viewing things, even more, perhaps, from being brought for a time under the influence of so noble and spiritual a mind.*"
—Athenæum.

THE CONSCIENCE: Lectures on Casuistry, delivered in the University of Cambridge. Second and Cheaper Edition. Crown 8vo. 5s.

The Saturday Review *says:* "*We rise from the perusal of these lectures with a detestation of all that is selfish and mean, and with a living impression that there is such a thing as goodness after all.*"

LECTURES ON THE ECCLESIASTICAL HISTORY OF THE FIRST AND SECOND CENTURIES. 8vo. 10s. 6d.

LEARNING AND WORKING. Six Lectures delivered in Willis's Rooms, London, in June and July, 1854.—THE RELIGION OF ROME, and its Influence on Modern Civilisation. Four Lectures delivered in the Philosophical Institution of Edinburgh, in December, 1854. Crown 8vo. 5s.

SERMONS PREACHED IN COUNTRY CHURCHES. Crown 8vo. 10s. 6d.

"*Earnest, practical, and extremely simple.*"—Literary Churchman. "*Good specimens of his simple and earnest eloquence. The Gospel incidents are realized with a vividness which we can well believe made the common people hear him gladly. Moreover they are sermons which must have done the hearers good.*"—John Bull.

Moorhouse.—Works by JAMES MOORHOUSE, M.A., Bishop of Melbourne:

SOME MODERN DIFFICULTIES RESPECTING the FACTS OF NATURE AND REVELATION. Fcap. 8vo. 2s. 6d.

JACOB. Three Sermons preached before the University of Cambridge in Lent 1870. Extra fcap. 8vo. 3s. 6d.

O'Brien.—PRAYER. Five Sermons preached in the Chapel of Trinity College, Dublin. By JAMES THOMAS O'BRIEN, D.D., Bishop of Ossory and Ferns. 8vo. 6s.

"*It is with much pleasure and satisfaction that we render our humble tribute to the value of a publication whose author deserves to be remembered with such deep respect.*"—Church Quarterly Review.

Palgrave.—HYMNS. By FRANCIS TURNER PALGRAVE. Third Edition, enlarged. 18mo. 1s. 6d.

This is a collection of twenty original Hymns, which the Literary Churchman *speaks of as "so choice, so perfect, and so refined,—so tender in feeling, and so scholarly in expression."*

Paul of Tarsus. An Inquiry into the Times and the Gospel of the Apostle of the Gentiles. By a GRADUATE. 8vo. 10s. 6d.

"*Turn where we will throughout the volume, we find the best fruit of patient inquiry, sound scholarship, logical argument, and fairness of conclusion. No thoughtful reader will rise from its perusal without a real and lasting profit to himself, and a sense of permanent addition to the cause of truth.*"—Standard.

Philochristus.—MEMOIRS OF A DISCIPLE OF THE LORD. Second Edition. 8vo. 12s.

"*The winning beauty of this book and the fascinating power with which the subject of it appeals to all English minds will secure for it many readers.*"—Contemporary Review.

Picton.—THE MYSTERY OF MATTER; and other Essays. By J. ALLANSON PICTON, Author of "New Theories and the Old Faith." Cheaper Edition. With New Preface. Crown 8vo. 6s.

Contents—The Mystery of Matter: The Philosophy of Ignorance: The Antithesis of Faith and Sight: The Essential Nature of Religion: Christian Pantheism.

Prescott.—THE THREEFOLD CORD. Sermons preached before the University of Cambridge. By J. E. PRESCOTT, B.D. Fcap. 8vo. 3s. 6d.

Procter.—A HISTORY OF THE BOOK OF COMMON PRAYER: With a Rationale of its Offices. By FRANCIS PROCTER, M.A. Thirteenth Edition, revised and enlarged. Crown 8vo. 10s. 6d.

The Athenæum *says:*—"*The origin of every part of the Prayer-book has been diligently investigated,—and there are few questions or facts connected with it which are not either sufficiently explained, or so referred to, that persons interested may work out the truth for themselves,*"

Procter and Maclear.—AN ELEMENTARY INTRODUCTION TO THE BOOK OF COMMON PRAYER. Re-arranged and Supplemented by an Explanation of the Morning and Evening Prayer and the Litany. By F. PROCTER, M.A. and G. F. MACLEAR, D.D. New Edition. Enlarged by the addition of the Communion Service and the Baptismal and Confirmation Offices. 18mo. 2s. 6d.

The Literary Churchman *characterizes it as "by far the completest and most satisfactory book of its kind we know. We wish it were in the hands of every schoolboy and every schoolmaster in the kingdom."*

Psalms of David CHRONOLOGICALLY ARRANGED. An Amended Version, with Historical Introductions and Explanatory Notes. By FOUR FRIENDS. Second and Cheaper Edition, much enlarged. Crown 8vo. 8s. 6d.

One of the chief designs of the Editors, in preparing this volume, was to restore the Psalter as far as possible to the order in which the Psalms were written. They give the division of each Psalm into strophes, and of each strophe into the lines which composed it, and amend the errors of translation. The Spectator *calls it "one of the most instructive and valuable books that have been published for many years."*

Psalter (Golden Treasury).—THE STUDENT'S EDITION. Being an Edition of the above with briefer Notes. 18mo. 3s. 6d.

The aim of this edition is simply to put the reader as far as possible in possession of the plain meaning of the writer. " It is a gem," the Nonconformist *says.*

Pulsford.—SERMONS PREACHED IN TRINITY CHURCH, GLASGOW. By WILLIAM PULSFORD, D.D. Cheaper Edition. Crown 8vo. 4s. 6d.

Ramsay.—THE CATECHISER'S MANUAL; or, the Church Catechism Illustrated and Explained, for the Use of Clergymen, Schoolmasters, and Teachers. By ARTHUR RAMSAY, M.A. Second Edition. 18mo. 1s. 6d.

Rays of Sunlight for Dark Days. A Book of Selections for the Suffering. With a Preface by C. J. VAUGHAN, D.D. 18mo. Eighth Edition. 3s. 6d. Also in morocco, old style.

Dr. Vaughan says in the Preface, after speaking of the general run of Books of Comfort for Mourners, "It is because I think that the little volume now offered to the Christian sufferer is one of greater wisdom and of deeper experience, that I have readily consented to the request that I would introduce it by a few words of Preface." The book consists of a series of very brief extracts from a great variety of authors, in prose and poetry, suited to the many moods of a mourning or suffering mind. "Mostly gems of the first water."—Clerical Journal.

Reynolds.—NOTES OF THE CHRISTIAN LIFE. A Selection of Sermons by HENRY ROBERT REYNOLDS, B.A., President of Cheshunt College, and Fellow of University College, London. Crown 8vo. 7s. 6d.

Roberts.—DISCUSSIONS ON THE GOSPELS. By the Rev. ALEXANDER ROBERTS, D.D. Second Edition, revised and enlarged. 8vo. 16s.

Robinson.—MAN IN THE IMAGE OF GOD; and other Sermons preached in the Chapel of the Magdalen, Streatham, 1874—76. By H. G. ROBINSON, M.A., Prebendary of York. Crown 8vo. 7s. 6d.

Romanes.—CHRISTIAN PRAYER AND GENERAL LAWS, being the Burney Prize Essay for 1873. With an Appendix, examining the views of Messrs. Knight, Robertson, Brooke, Tyndall, and Galton. By GEORGE J. ROMANES, M.A. Crown 8vo. 5s.

Salmon.—THE REIGN OF LAW, and other Sermons, preached in the Chapel of Trinity College, Dublin. By the Rev. GEORGE SALMON, D.D., Regius Professor of Divinity in the University of Dublin. Crown 8vo. 6s.

"Well considered, learned, and powerful discourses."—Spectator.

Sanday.—THE GOSPELS IN THE SECOND CENTURY. An Examination of the Critical part of a Work entitled "Supernatural Religion." By WILLIAM SANDAY, M.A., late Fellow of Trinity College, Oxford. Crown 8vo. 8s. 6d.

"A very important book for the critical side of the question as to the authenticity of the New Testament, and it is hardly possible to conceive a writer of greater fairness, candour, and scrupulousness."—Spectator.

Selborne.—THE BOOK OF PRAISE: From the Best English Hymn Writers. Selected and arranged by Lord SELBORNE. With Vignette by WOOLNER. 18mo. 4s. 6d.

SELBORNE (Lord)—*continued.*

It has been the Editor's desire and aim to adhere strictly, in all cases in which it could be ascertained, to the genuine uncorrupted text of the authors themselves. The names of the authors and date of composition of the hymns, when known, are affixed, while notes are added to the volume, giving further details. The Hymns are arranged according to subjects. " There is not room for two opinions as to the value of the 'Book of Praise.'"
—Guardian. *"Approaches as nearly as one can conceive to perfection."*
—Nonconformist.

BOOK OF PRAISE HYMNAL. *See* end of this Catalogue.

Service.—SALVATION HERE AND HEREAFTER. Sermons and Essays. By the Rev. JOHN SERVICE, D.D., Minister of Inch. Fourth Edition. Crown 8vo. 6s.

"We have enjoyed to-day a rare pleasure, having just closed a volume of sermons which rings true metal from title page to finis, and proves that another and very powerful recruit has been added to that small band of ministers of the Gospel who are not only abreast of the religious thought of their time, but have faith enough and courage enough to handle the questions which are the most critical, and stir men's minds most deeply, with frankness and thoroughness."—Spectator.

Shipley.—A THEORY ABOUT SIN, in relation to some Facts of Daily Life. Lent Lectures on the Seven Deadly Sins. By the Rev. ORBY SHIPLEY, M.A. Crown 8vo. 7s. 6d.

"Two things Mr. Shipley has done, and each of them is of considerable worth. He has grouped these sins afresh on a philosophic principle..... and he has applied the touchstone to the facts of our moral life... so wisely and so searchingly as to constitute his treatise a powerful antidote to self-deception."—Literary Churchman.

Smith.—PROPHECY A PREPARATION FOR CHRIST. Eight Lectures preached before the University of Oxford, being the Bampton Lectures for 1869. By R. PAYNE SMITH, D.D., Dean of Canterbury. Second and Cheaper Edition. Crown 8vo. 6s.

The author's object in these Lectures is to shew that there exists in the Old Testament an element, which no criticism on naturalistic principles can either account for or explain away: that element is Prophecy. The author endeavours to prove that its force does not consist merely in its predictions. "These Lectures overflow with solid learning."—Record.

Smith.—CHRISTIAN FAITH. Sermons preached before the University of Cambridge. By W. SAUMAREZ SMITH, M.A., Principal of St. Aidan's College, Birkenhead. Fcap. 8vo. 3s. 6d.

Stanley.—Works by the Very Rev. A. P. STANLEY, D.D., Dean of Westminster:

THE ATHANASIAN CREED, with a Preface on the General Recommendations of the RITUAL COMMISSION. Cr. 8vo. 2s.

"Dr. Stanley puts with admirable force the objections which may be made to the Creed; equally admirable, we think, in his statement of its advantages."—Spectator.

THE NATIONAL THANKSGIVING. Sermons preached in Westminster Abbey. Second Edition. Crown 8vo. 2s. 6d.

ADDRESSES AND SERMONS AT ST. ANDREW'S in 1872, 1875 and 1876. Crown 8vo. 5s.

Stewart and Tait.—THE UNSEEN UNIVERSE; or, Physical Speculations on a Future State. By Professors BALFOUR STEWART and P. G. TAIT. Sixth Edition, Revised and Enlarged. Crown 8vo. 6s.

"A most remarkable and most interesting volume, which, probably more than any that has appeared in modern times, will affect religious thought on many momentous questions—insensibly it may be, but very largely and very beneficially."—Church Quarterly. *"This book is one which well deserves the attention of thoughtful and religious readers...... It is a perfectly safe enquiry, on scientific grounds, into the possibilities of a future existence."*—Guardian.

Swainson.—Works by C. A. SWAINSON, D.D., Canon of Chichester:

THE CREEDS OF THE CHURCH in their Relations to Holy Scripture and the Conscience of the Christian 8vo. cloth. 9s.

THE AUTHORITY OF THE NEW TESTAMENT, and other LECTURES, delivered before the University of Cambridge. 8vo. cloth. 12s.

Taylor.—THE RESTORATION OF BELIEF. New and Revised Edition. By ISAAC TAYLOR, Esq. Crown 8vo. 8s. 6d.

Temple.—SERMONS PREACHED IN THE CHAPEL of RUGBY SCHOOL. By F. TEMPLE, D.D., Bishop of Exeter. New and Cheaper Edition. Extra fcap. 8vo. 4s. 6d.

This volume contains Thirty-five Sermons on topics more or less intimately connected with every-day life. The following are a few of the subjects discoursed upon:—"Love and Duty;" "Coming to Christ;"

TEMPLE (Dr.)—*continued.*

"*Great Men;*" "*Faith;*" "*Doubts;*" "*Scruples;*" "*Original Sin;*" "*Friendship;*" "*Helping Others;*" "*The Discipline of Temptation;*" "*Strength a Duty;*" "*Worldliness;*" "*Ill Temper;*" "*The Burial of the Past.*"

A SECOND SERIES OF SERMONS PREACHED IN THE CHAPEL OF RUGBY SCHOOL. Second Edition. Extra fcap. 8vo. 6s.

This Second Series of Forty-two brief, pointed, practical Sermons, on topics intimately connected with the every-day life of young and old, will be acceptable to all who are acquainted with the First Series. The following are a few of the subjects treated of:—"*Disobedience,*" "*Almsgiving,*" "*The Unknown Guidance of God,*" "*Apathy one of our Trials,*" "*High Aims in Leaders,*" "*Doing our Best,*" "*The Use of Knowledge,*" "*Use of Observances,*" "*Martha and Mary,*" "*John the Baptist,*" "*Severity before Mercy,*" "*Even Mistakes Punished,*" "*Morality and Religion,*" "*Children,*" "*Action the Test of Spiritual Life,*" "*Self-Respect,*" "*Too Late,*" "*The Tercentenary.*"

A THIRD SERIES OF SERMONS PREACHED IN RUGBY SCHOOL CHAPEL IN 1867—1869. Extra fcap. 8vo. 6s.

This third series of Bishop Temple's Rugby Sermons, contains thirty-six brief discourses, including the " Good-bye" sermon preached on his leaving Rugby to enter on the office he now holds.

Thring.—Works by Rev. EDWARD THRING, M.A.:

SERMONS DELIVERED AT UPPINGHAM SCHOOL. Crown 8vo. 5s.

THOUGHTS ON LIFE-SCIENCE. New Edition, enlarged and revised. Crown 8vo. 7s. 6d.

Trench.—Works by R. CHENEVIX TRENCH, D.D., Archbishop of Dublin:

NOTES ON THE PARABLES OF OUR LORD. Thirteenth Edition. 8vo. 12s.

This work has taken its place as a standard exposition and interpretation of Christ's Parables. The book is prefaced by an Introductory Essay in four chapters:—I. On the definition of the Parable. II. On Teaching by Parables. III. On the Interpretation of the Parables. IV. On other Parables besides those in the Scriptures. The author then proceeds to take up the Parables one by one, and by the aid of philology, history, antiquities, and the researches of travellers, shews forth the significance,

TRENCH (Archbishop)—*continued.*

beauty, and applicability of each, concluding with what he deems its true moral interpretation. In the numerous Notes are many valuable references, illustrative quotations, critical and philological annotations, etc., and appended to the volume is a classified list of fifty-six works on the Parables.

NOTES ON THE MIRACLES OF OUR LORD. Eleventh Edition, revised. 8vo. 12s.

In the 'Preliminary Essay' to this work, all the momentous and interesting questions that have been raised in connection with Miracles, are discussed with considerable fulness. The Essay consists of six chapters:— I. On the Names of Miracles, i.e. the Greek words by which they are designated in the New Testament. II. The Miracles and Nature—What is the difference between a Miracle and any event in the ordinary course of Nature? III. The Authority of Miracles—Is the Miracle to command absolute obedience? IV. The Evangelical, compared with the other cycles of Miracles. V. The Assaults on the Miracles—1. The Jewish. 2. The Heathen (Celsus etc.). 3. The Pantheistic (Spinosa etc.). 4. The Sceptical (Hume). 5. The Miracles only relatively miraculous (Schleiermacher). 6. The Rationalistic (Paulus). 7. The Historico-Critical (Woolston, Strauss). VI. The Apologetic Worth of the Miracles. The author then treats the separate Miracles as he does the Parables.

SYNONYMS OF THE NEW TESTAMENT. Eighth Edition, enlarged. 8vo. cloth. 12s.

This Edition has been carefully revised, and a considerable number of new Synonyms added. Appended is an Index to the Synonyms, and an Index to many other words alluded to or explained throughout the work. "He is," the Athenæum *says, "a guide in this department of knowledge to whom his readers may intrust themselves with confidence. His sober judgment and sound sense are barriers against the misleading influence of arbitrary hypotheses."*

ON THE AUTHORIZED VERSION OF THE NEW TESTAMENT. Second Edition. 8vo. 7s.

After some Introductory Remarks, in which the propriety of a revision is briefly discussed, the whole question of the merits of the present version is gone into in detail, in eleven chapters. Appended is a chronological list of works bearing on the subject, an Index of the principal Texts considered, an Index of Greek Words, and an Index of other Words referred to throughout the book.

STUDIES IN THE GOSPELS. Fourth Edition, revised. 8vo. 10s. 6d.

This book is published under the conviction that the assertion often made is untrue,—viz. that the Gospels are in the main plain and easy,

TRENCH (Archbishop)—*continued*.

and that all the chief difficulties of the New Testament are to be found in the Epistles. These "Studies," sixteen in number, are the fruit of a much larger scheme, and each Study deals with some important episode mentioned in the Gospels, in a critical, philosophical, and practical manner. Many references and quotations are added to the Notes. Among the subjects treated are:—*The Temptation; Christ and the Samaritan Woman; The Three Aspirants; The Transfiguration; Zacchæus; The True Vine; The Penitent Malefactor; Christ and the Two Disciples on the way to Emmaus.*

COMMENTARY ON THE EPISTLES to the SEVEN CHURCHES IN ASIA. Third Edition, revised. 8vo. 8s. 6d.

The present work consists of an Introduction, being a commentary on Rev. i. 4—20, a detailed examination of each of the Seven Epistles, in all its bearings, and an Excursus on the Historico-Prophetical Interpretation of the Epistles.

THE SERMON ON THE MOUNT. An Exposition drawn from the writings of St. Augustine, with an Essay on his merits as an Interpreter of Holy Scripture. Third Edition, enlarged. 8vo. 10s. 6d.

The first half of the present work consists of a dissertation in eight chapters on "Augustine as an Interpreter of Scripture," the titles of the several chapters being as follow:—*I. Augustine's General Views of Scripture and its Interpretation. II. The External Helps for the Interpretation of Scripture possessed by Augustine. III. Augustine's Principles and Canons of Interpretation. IV. Augustine's Allegorical Interpretation of Scripture. V. Illustrations of Augustine's Skill as an Interpreter of Scripture. VI. Augustine on John the Baptist and on St. Stephen. VII. Augustine on the Epistle to the Romans. VIII. Miscellaneous Examples of Augustine's Interpretation of Scripture.* The latter half of the work consists of Augustine's Exposition of the Sermon on the Mount, not however a mere series of quotations from Augustine, but a connected account of his sentiments on the various passages of that Sermon, interspersed with criticisms by Archbishop Trench.

SHIPWRECKS OF FAITH. Three Sermons preached before the University of Cambridge in May, 1867. Fcap. 8vo. 2s. 6d.

These Sermons are especially addressed to young men. The subjects are "Balaam," "Saul," and "Judas Iscariot." These lives are set forth as beacon-lights, "to warn us off from perilous reefs and quicksands, which have been the destruction of many, and which might only too easily be ours." *The* John Bull *says*, "they are, like all he writes, affectionate and earnest discourses."

TRENCH (Archbishop)—*continued.*

SERMONS Preached for the most part in Ireland. 8vo. 10s. 6d.

This volume consists of Thirty-two Sermons, the greater part of which were preached in Ireland; the subjects are as follow:—Jacob, a Prince with God and with Men—Agrippa—The Woman that was a Sinner—Secret Faults—The Seven Worse Spirits—Freedom in the Truth—Joseph and his Brethren—Bearing one another's Burdens—Christ's Challenge to the World—The Love of Money—The Salt of the Earth—The Armour of God—Light in the Lord—The Jailer of Philippi—The Thorn in the Flesh—Isaiah's Vision—Selfishness—Abraham interceding for Sodom—Vain Thoughts—Pontius Pilate—The Brazen Serpent—The Death and Burial of Moses—A Word from the Cross—The Church's Worship in the Beauty of Holiness—Every Good Gift from Above—On the Hearing of Prayer—The Kingdom which cometh not with Observation—Pressing towards the Mark—Saul—The Good Shepherd—The Valley of Dry Bones—All Saints.

LECTURES ON MEDIEVAL CHURCH HISTORY. Being the Substance of Lectures delivered in Queen's College, London. 8vo. 12s.

Contents:—The Middle Ages Beginning—The Conversion of England—Islam—The Conversion of Germany—The Iconoclasts—The Crusades—The Papacy at its Height—The Sects of the Middle Ages—The Mendicant Orders—The Waldenses—The Revival of Learning—Christian Art in the Middle Ages, &c., &c.

Tulloch.—THE CHRIST OF THE GOSPELS AND THE CHRIST OF MODERN CRITICISM. Lectures on M. RENAN's "Vie de Jésus." By JOHN TULLOCH, D.D., Principal of the College of St. Mary, in the University of St. Andrew's. Extra fcap. 8vo. 4s. 6d.

Vaughan.—Works by CHARLES J. VAUGHAN, D.D., Master of the Temple:

CHRIST SATISFYING THE INSTINCTS OF HUMANITY. Eight Lectures delivered in the Temple Church. Second Edition. Extra fcap. 8vo. 3s. 6d.

"We are convinced that there are congregations, in number unmistakably increasing, to whom such Essays as these, full of thought and learning, are infinitely more beneficial, for they are more acceptable, than the recognised type of sermons."—John Bull.

THE BOOK AND THE LIFE, and other Sermons, preached before the University of Cambridge. Third Edition. Fcap. 8vo. 4s. 6d.

VAUGHAN (Dr. C. J.)—*continued.*

TWELVE DISCOURSES on SUBJECTS CONNECTED WITH THE LITURGY and WORSHIP of the CHURCH OF ENGLAND. Fcap. 8vo. 6s.

LESSONS OF LIFE AND GODLINESS. A Selection of Sermons preached in the Parish Church of Doncaster. Fourth and Cheaper Edition. Fcap. 8vo. 3s. 6d.

This volume consists of Nineteen Sermons, mostly on subjects connected with the every-day walk and conversation of Christians. The Spectator *styles them "earnest and human. They are adapted to every class and order in the social system, and will be read with wakeful interest by all who seek to amend whatever may be amiss in their natural disposition or in their acquired habits."*

WORDS FROM THE GOSPELS. A Second Selection of Sermons preached in the Parish Church of Doncaster. Third Edition. Fcap. 8vo. 4s. 6d.

The Nonconformist *characterises these Sermons as "of practical earnestness, of a thoughtfulness that penetrates the common conditions and experiences of life, and brings the truths and examples of Scripture to bear on them with singular force, and of a style that owes its real elegance to the simplicity and directness which have fine culture for their roots."*

LIFE'S WORK AND GOD'S DISCIPLINE. Three Sermons. Third Edition. Fcap. 8vo. 2s. 6d.

THE WHOLESOME WORDS OF JESUS CHRIST. Four Sermons preached before the University of Cambridge in November 1866. Second Edition. Fcap. 8vo. 3s. 6d.

Dr. Vaughan uses the word "Wholesome" here in its literal and original sense, the sense in which St. Paul uses it, as meaning healthy, sound, conducing to right living; and in these Sermons he points out and illustrates several of the "wholesome" characteristics of the Gospel, —the Words of Christ. The John Bull *says this volume is "replete with all the author's well-known vigour of thought and richness of expression."*

FOES OF FAITH. Sermons preached before the University of Cambridge in November 1868. Second Edition. Fcap. 8vo. 3s. 6d.

The "Foes of Faith" preached against in these Four Sermons are:— I. "Unreality." II. "Indolence." III. "Irreverence." IV. "Inconsistency."

LECTURES ON THE EPISTLE to the PHILIPPIANS. Third and Cheaper Edition. Extra fcap. 8vo. 5s.

Each Lecture is prefaced by a literal translation from the Greek of the paragraph which forms its subject, contains first a minute explanation

VAUGHAN (Dr. C. J.)—*continued.*

of the passage on which it is based, and then a practical application of the verse or clause selected as its text.

LECTURES ON THE REVELATION OF ST. JOHN.
Fourth Edition. Two Vols. Extra fcap. 8vo. 9s.

In this Edition of these Lectures, the literal translations of the passages expounded will be found interwoven in the body of the Lectures themselves. "Dr. Vaughan's Sermons," the Spectator *says, "are the most practical discourses on the Apocalypse with which we are acquainted." Prefixed is a Synopsis of the Book of Revelation, and appended is an Index of passages illustrating the language of the Book.*

EPIPHANY, LENT, AND EASTER. A Selection of
Expository Sermons. Third Edition. Crown 8vo. 10s. 6d.

THE EPISTLES OF ST. PAUL. For English Readers.
PART I., containing the FIRST EPISTLE TO THE THESSALONIANS. Second Edition. 8vo. 1s. 6d.

It is the object of this work to enable English readers, unacquainted with Greek, to enter with intelligence into the meaning, connection, and phraseology of the writings of the great Apostle.

ST. PAUL'S EPISTLE TO THE ROMANS. The Greek
Text, with English Notes. Fourth Edition. Crown 8vo. 7s. 6d.

The Guardian *says of the work,*—*"For educated young men his commentary seems to fill a gap hitherto unfilled. . . . As a whole, Dr. Vaughan appears to us to have given to the world a valuable book of original and careful and earnest thought bestowed on the accomplishment of a work which will be of much service and which is much needed."*

THE CHURCH OF THE FIRST DAYS.
Series I.   The Church of Jerusalem.   Third Edition.
"   II.   The Church of the Gentiles.   Third Edition.
"   III.   The Church of the World.   Third Edition.
Fcap. 8vo. 4s. 6d. each.

The British Quarterly *says, "These Sermons are worthy of all praise, and are models of pulpit teaching."*

COUNSELS for YOUNG STUDENTS. Three Sermons
preached before the University of Cambridge at the Opening of the Academical Year 1870-71. Fcap. 8vo. 2s. 6d.

The titles of the Three Sermons contained in this volume are:—*I. "The Great Decision." II. "The House and the Builder." III. "The Prayer and the Counter-Prayer." They all bear pointedly, earnestly, and sympathisingly upon the conduct and pursuits of young students and young men generally.*

VAUGHAN (Dr. C. J.)—*continued.*

NOTES FOR LECTURES ON CONFIRMATION, with suitable Prayers. Tenth Edition. Fcap. 8vo. 1s. 6d.

THE TWO GREAT TEMPTATIONS. The Temptation of Man, and the Temptation of Christ. Lectures delivered in the Temple Church, Lent 1872. Second Edition. Extra fcap. 8vo. 3s. 6d.

WORDS FROM THE CROSS: Lent Lectures, 1875; and Thoughts for these Times: University Sermons, 1874. Extra fcap. 8vo. 4s. 6d.

ADDRESSES TO YOUNG CLERGYMEN, delivered at Salisbury in September and October, 1875. Extra fcap. 8vo. 4s. 6d.

HEROES OF FAITH: Lectures on Hebrews xi. Extra fcap. 8vo. 6s.

THE YOUNG LIFE EQUIPPING ITSELF FOR GOD'S SERVICE: Sermons before the University of Cambridge. Sixth Edition. Extra fcap. 8vo. 3s. 6d.

THE SOLIDITY OF TRUE RELIGION; and other Sermons. Second Edition. Extra fcap. 8vo. 3s. 6d.

WORDS OF HOPE from the Pulpit of the Temple Church. Fourth Edition. Extra fcap. 8vo. 5s.

SERMONS IN HARROW SCHOOL CHAPEL (1847). 8vo. 10s. 6d.

NINE SERMONS IN HARROW SCHOOL CHAPEL (1849). Fcap. 8vo. 5s.

"SON, GIVE ME THY HEART," SERMONS. Extra Fcap. 8vo. [*Nearly ready.*

Vaughan (E. T.)—SOME REASONS OF OUR CHRISTIAN HOPE. Hulsean Lectures for 1875. By E. T. VAUGHAN, M.A., Rector of Harpenden. Crown 8vo. 6s. 6d.

"*His words are those of a well-tried scholar and a sound theologian, and they will be read widely and valued deeply by an audience far beyond the range of that which listened to their masterly pleading at Cambridge.*"
—Standard.

Vaughan (D. J.)—Works by CANON VAUGHAN, of Leicester:

SERMONS PREACHED IN ST. JOHN'S CHURCH, LEICESTER, during the Years 1855 and 1856. Cr. 8vo. 5s. 6d.

VAUGHAN (D. J.)—*continued.*

CHRISTIAN EVIDENCES AND THE BIBLE. New Edition, revised and enlarged. Fcap. 8vo. cloth. 5s. 6d.

THE PRESENT TRIAL OF FAITH. Sermons preached in St. Martin's Church, Leicester. Crown 8vo. 9s.

Venn.—ON SOME OF THE CHARACTERISTICS OF BELIEF, Scientific and Religious. Being the Hulsean Lectures for 1869. By the Rev. J. VENN, M.A. 8vo. 6s. 6d.

These discourses are intended to illustrate, explain, and work out into some of their consequences, certain characteristics by which the attainment of religious belief is prominently distinguished from the attainment of belief upon most other subjects.

Warington.—THE WEEK OF CREATION; or, The Cosmogony of Genesis considered in its Relation to Modern Science. By GEORGE WARINGTON, Author of "The Historic Character of the Pentateuch Vindicated." Crown 8vo. 4s. 6d.

"A very able vindication of the Mosaic Cosmogony by a writer who unites the advantages of a critical knowledge of the Hebrew text and of distinguished scientific attainments."—Spectator.

Westcott.—Works by BROOKE FOSS WESTCOTT, D.D., Regius Professor of Divinity in the University of Cambridge; Canon of Peterborough:

The London Quarterly, *speaking of Mr. Westcott, says,* "*To a learning and accuracy which command respect and confidence, he unites what are not always to be found in union with these qualities, the no less valuable faculties of lucid arrangement and graceful and facile expression.*"

AN INTRODUCTION TO THE STUDY OF THE GOSPELS. Fifth Edition. Crown 8vo. 10s. 6d.

The author's chief object in this work has been to shew that there is a true mean between the idea of a formal harmonization of the Gospels and the abandonment of their absolute truth. After an Introduction on the General Effects of the course of Modern Philosophy on the popular views of Christianity, he proceeds to determine in what way the principles therein indicated may be applied to the study of the Gospels.

A GENERAL SURVEY OF THE HISTORY OF THE CANON OF THE NEW TESTAMENT during the First Four Centuries. Fourth Edition, revised, with a Preface on "Supernatural Religion." Crown 8vo. 10s. 6d.

The object of this treatise is to deal with the New Testament as a whole, and that on purely historical grounds. The separate books of which it is

WESTCOTT (Dr.)—*continued.*

composed are considered not individually, but as claiming to be parts of the apostolic heritage of Christians. The Author has thus endeavoured to connect the history of the New Testament Canon with the growth and consolidation of the Catholic Church, and to point out the relation existing between the amount of evidence for the authenticity of its component parts and the whole mass of Christian literature. "The treatise," says the British Quarterly, "is a scholarly performance, learned, dispassionate, discriminating, worthy of his subject and of the present state of Christian literature in relation to it."

THE BIBLE IN THE CHURCH. A Popular Account of the Collection and Reception of the Holy Scriptures in the Christian Churches. Sixth Edition. 18mo. 4s. 6d.

A GENERAL VIEW OF THE HISTORY OF THE ENGLISH BIBLE. Second Edition. Crown 8vo. 10s. 6d.

The Pall Mall Gazette *calls the work "A brief, scholarly, and, to a great extent, an original contribution to theological literature."*

THE CHRISTIAN LIFE, MANIFOLD AND ONE. Six Sermons preached in Peterborough Cathedral. Crown 8vo. 2s. 6d.

The Six Sermons contained in this volume are the first preached by the author as a Canon of Peterborough Cathedral. The subjects are:— I. "Life consecrated by the Ascension." II. "Many Gifts, One Spirit." III. "The Gospel of the Resurrection." IV. "Sufficiency of God." V. "Action the Test of Faith." VI. "Progress from the Confession of God."

THE GOSPEL OF THE RESURRECTION. Thoughts on its Relation to Reason and History. Third Edition, enlarged. Crown 8vo. 6s.

The present Essay is an endeavour to consider some of the elementary truths of Christianity, as a miraculous Revelation, from the side of History and Reason. The author endeavours to shew that a devout belief in the Life of Christ is quite compatible with a broad view of the course of human progress and a frank trust in the laws of our own minds. In the third edition the author has carefully reconsidered the whole argument, and by the help of several kind critics has been enabled to correct some faults and to remove some ambiguities, which had been overlooked before.

ON THE RELIGIOUS OFFICE OF THE UNIVERSITIES. Crown 8vo. 4s. 6d.

"There is certainly no man of our time—no man at least who has obtained the command of the public ear—whose utterances can compare with those of Professor Westcott for largeness of views and comprehensiveness of

grasp...... There is wisdom, and truth, and thought enough, and a harmony and mutual connection running through them all, which makes the collection of more real value than many an ambitious treatise."—Literary Churchman.

Wilkins.—THE LIGHT OF THE WORLD. An Essay, by A. S. WILKINS, M.A., Professor of Latin in Owens College, Manchester. Second Edition. Crown 8vo. 3s. 6d.

"It would be difficult to praise too highly the spirit, the burden, the conclusions, or the scholarly finish of this beautiful Essay."—British Quarterly Review.

Wilson.—THE BIBLE STUDENT'S GUIDE TO THE MORE CORRECT UNDERSTANDING of the ENGLISH TRANSLATION OF THE OLD TESTAMENT, by Reference to the Original Hebrew. By WILLIAM WILSON, D.D., Canon of Winchester. Second Edition, carefully revised. 4to. 25s.

"The author believes that the present work is the nearest approach to a complete Concordance of every word in the original that has yet been made: and as a Concordance, it may be found of great use to the Bible student, while at the same time it serves the important object of furnishing the means of comparing synonymous words, and of eliciting their precise and distinctive meaning. The knowledge of the Hebrew language is not absolutely necessary to the profitable use of the work. The plan of the work is simple: every word occurring in the English Version is arranged alphabetically, and under it is given the Hebrew word or words, with a full explanation of their meaning, of which it is meant to be a translation, and a complete list of the passages where it occurs. Following the general work is a complete Hebrew and English Index, which is, in effect, a Hebrew-English Dictionary."

Worship (The) of God and Fellowship among Men. Sermons on Public Worship. By Professor MAURICE, and others. Fcap. 8vo. 3s. 6d.

Yonge (Charlotte M.)—Works by CHARLOTTE M. YONGE, Author of "The Heir of Redclyffe:"

SCRIPTURE READINGS FOR SCHOOLS AND FAMILIES. Globe 8vo. 1s. 6d. With Comments, 3s. 6d.

SECOND SERIES. From Joshua to Solomon. Extra fcap. 8vo. 1s. 6d. With Comments, 3s. 6d.

THIRD SERIES. The Kings and Prophets. Extra fcap. 8vo. 1s. 6d. With Comments, 3s. 6d.

FOURTH SERIES. The Gospel Times. Extra fcap. 8vo. 1s. 6d. With Comments, 3s. 6d.

YONGE (Charlotte M.)—*continued.*

Actual need has led the author to endeavour to prepare a reading book convenient for study with children, containing the very words of the Bible, with only a few expedient omissions, and arranged in Lessons of such length as by experience she has found to suit with children's ordinary power of accurate attentive interest. The verse form has been retained because of its convenience for children reading in class, and as more resembling their Bibles; but the poetical portions have been given in their lines. Professor Huxley at a meeting of the London School-board, particularly mentioned the Selection made by Miss Yonge, as an example of how selections might be made for School reading. "Her Comments are models of their kind."—Literary Churchman.

THE PUPILS OF ST. JOHN THE DIVINE. New Edition. Crown 8vo. 6s.

"Young and old will be equally refreshed and taught by these pages, in which nothing is dull, and nothing is far-fetched."—Churchman.

PIONEERS AND FOUNDERS; or, Recent Workers in the Mission Field. With Frontispiece and Vignette Portrait of Bishop HEBER. Crown 8vo. 6s.

The missionaries whose biographies are here given, are—John Eliot, the Apostle of the Red Indians; David Brainerd, the Enthusiast; Christian F. Schwartz, the Councillor of Tanjore; Henry Martyn, the Scholar-Missionary; William Carey and Joshua Marshman, the Serampore Missionaries; the Judson Family; the Bishops of Calcutta—Thomas Middleton, Reginald Heber, Daniel Wilson; Samuel Marsden, the Australian Chaplain and Friend of the Maori; John Williams, the Martyr of Erromango; Allen Gardener, the Sailor Martyr; Charles Frederick Mackenzie, the Martyr of Zambesi.

THE "BOOK OF PRAISE" HYMNAL,

COMPILED AND ARRANGED BY
LORD SELBORNE.

In the following four forms:—

A. Beautifully printed in Royal 32mo., limp cloth, price 6d.
B.   ,,   ,,   Small 18mo., larger type, cloth limp, 1s.
C. Same edition on fine paper, cloth, 1s. 6d.
Also an edition with Music, selected, harmonized, and composed by **JOHN HULLAH**, in square 18mo., cloth, 3s. 6d.

The large acceptance which has been given to "The Book of Praise" by all classes of Christian people encourages the Publishers in entertaining the hope that this Hymnal, which is mainly selected from it, may be extensively used in Congregations, and in some degree at least meet the desires of those who seek uniformity in common worship as a means towards that unity which pious souls yearn after, and which our Lord prayed for in behalf of his Church. "The office of a hymn is not to teach controversial Theology, but to give the voice of song to practical religion. No doubt, to do this, it must embody sound doctrine; but it ought to do so, not after the manner of the schools, but with the breadth, freedom, and simplicity of the Fountain-head." On this principle has Sir R. Palmer proceeded in the preparation of this book.

The arrangement adopted is the following:—

PART I. consists of *Hymns arranged according to the subjects of the Creed*—"God the Creator," "Christ Incarnate," "Christ Crucified," "Christ Risen," "Christ Ascended," "Christ's Kingdom and Judgment," etc.

PART II. *comprises Hymns arranged according to the subjects of the Lord's Prayer.*

PART III. *Hymns for natural and sacred seasons.*

There are 320 *Hymns in all.*

CAMBRIDGE:—PRINTED BY J. PALMER.

www.ingramcontent.com/pod-product-compliance
Lightning Source LLC
Chambersburg PA
CBHW030012240426
43672CB00007B/921